SpringerBriefs in Applied Sciences and Technology

Computational Intelligence

Series Editor

Janusz Kacprzyk, Systems Research Institute, Polish Academy of Sciences, Warsaw, Poland

SpringerBriefs in Computational Intelligence are a series of slim high-quality publications encompassing the entire spectrum of Computational Intelligence. Featuring compact volumes of 50 to 125 pages (approximately 20,000-45,000 words), Briefs are shorter than a conventional book but longer than a journal article. Thus Briefs serve as timely, concise tools for students, researchers, and professionals.

Surekha Borra · Nilanjan Dey · Sheng-Lung Peng

AIoT Deployment in Business Evolution

Sociotechnical Readiness and Human-Centric Strategies

Surekha Borra
Department of Computer Science
and Engineering (IoT
Cybersecurity and Blockchain Technology)
K. S. Institute of Technology
Bengaluru, Karnataka, India

Nilanjan Dey
Department of Computer Science
and Engineering
Techno International New Town
Kolkata, West Bengal, India

Sheng-Lung Peng
Department of Creative Technologies
and Product Design
School of Innovative Design
and Management
National Tapei University of Business
Taipei, Taiwan

ISSN 2191-530X ISSN 2191-5318 (electronic)
SpringerBriefs in Applied Sciences and Technology
ISSN 2625-3704 ISSN 2625-3712 (electronic)
SpringerBriefs in Computational Intelligence
ISBN 978-3-032-09471-1 ISBN 978-3-032-09472-8 (eBook)
https://doi.org/10.1007/978-3-032-09472-8

© The Editor(s) (if applicable) and The Author(s), under exclusive license to Springer Nature Switzerland AG 2026

This work is subject to copyright. All rights are solely and exclusively licensed by the Publisher, whether the whole or part of the material is concerned, specifically the rights of translation, reprinting, reuse of illustrations, recitation, broadcasting, reproduction on microfilms or in any other physical way, and transmission or information storage and retrieval, electronic adaptation, computer software, or by similar or dissimilar methodology now known or hereafter developed.

The use of general descriptive names, registered names, trademarks, service marks, etc. in this publication does not imply, even in the absence of a specific statement, that such names are exempt from the relevant protective laws and regulations and therefore free for general use.

The publisher, the authors and the editors are safe to assume that the advice and information in this book are believed to be true and accurate at the date of publication. Neither the publisher nor the authors or the editors give a warranty, expressed or implied, with respect to the material contained herein or for any errors or omissions that may have been made. The publisher remains neutral with regard to jurisdictional claims in published maps and institutional affiliations.

This Springer imprint is published by the registered company Springer Nature Switzerland AG
The registered company address is: Gewerbestrasse 11, 6330 Cham, Switzerland

If disposing of this product, please recycle the paper.

Preface

The integration of artificial intelligence (AI) with the Internet of Things (IoT), known as the AIoT, is recognized for its transformative potential across various sectors by enhancing automation, efficiency, and decision-making capabilities. The evolution from isolated digital initiatives to integrated AIoT ecosystems demands a significant shift in thinking—not only about how technology is developed and deployed but also about how it is governed, experienced, and continuously improved. It is no longer sufficient to pursue AIoT purely from a technical or efficiency standpoint. Success in this domain hinges on a holistic approach that harmonizes innovation with ethical responsibility, inclusivity, collaboration, and long-term value creation.

The book delves into the technological, human, and organizational dimensions of deploying AIoT systems, highlighting the importance of sociotechnical readiness and human-centric approaches to ensure sustainable and ethical business transformation. While many discussions about AIoT mainly focus on technology, data, or market opportunities, this book also emphasizes the human, cultural, and governance factors that can greatly influence whether these systems succeed or fail in real life.

This book is written for a diverse audience: business leaders seeking to align AIoT with strategic objectives, technologists aiming to design robust and scalable systems, policymakers grappling with regulation and ethical concerns, and researchers exploring the future of sociotechnical integration. Each group will find insights tailored to their perspective, but the central theme remains constant: AIoT is not only about technology but also about people, organizations, and the values we embed into digital systems.

The chapters are organized to guide the reader from foundational understanding toward strategic foresight. Beginning with the historical trajectories of AI and IoT and their convergence, the text progresses through system architectures, deployment strategies, governance frameworks, and design philosophies before turning to long-term value creation and emerging trends. Readers may choose to follow the full arc sequentially or engage with individual chapters for focused exploration.

Chapter 1 sets the stage by tracing the historical development of IoT and AI as independent technologies. It then explores their convergence into AIoT, marking a paradigm shift in business innovation. This chapter also introduces the sociotechnical aspects of this convergence, emphasizing the interplay between technology, people, and organizations.

Chapter 2 breaks down the core architecture of AIoT systems, detailing components such as edge devices, cloud infrastructure, and intelligent analytics. Real-world applications are discussed across industries—manufacturing, healthcare, smart cities, and retail—followed by a review of AIoT's strategic benefits, including operational efficiency, data-driven decision-making, and customer engagement.

Chapter 3 focuses on practical deployment strategies and the multifaceted challenges that businesses face. It covers strategic planning for AIoT adoption, technical hurdles such as integration and interoperability, and the human-centric challenges involving culture, skills, and change resistance. The chapter introduces the concept of sociotechnical readiness as a critical success factor.

Chapter 4 presents a structured, step-by-step AIoT deployment framework covering defining objectives, assessing capabilities, creating a robust data strategy, fostering cross-functional collaboration, and selecting appropriate technologies. Human-centric concerns like skill development, ethical considerations, user experience design, and sustainable scaling are woven into the framework, making it both comprehensive and adaptable.

Chapter 5 addresses governance models and frameworks for monitoring and accountability, with a focus on data privacy, security, and regulatory compliance. Change management strategies are provided to facilitate smooth transitions, emphasizing leadership, communication, and stakeholder engagement.

Chapter 6 explores design philosophies such as Human-Centred AI, transparency, inclusivity, and accessibility. It also addresses the delicate balance between personalization and privacy and encourages participatory approaches through co-creation and iterative design processes.

Chapter 7 links AIoT with long-term strategic goals by examining how hyper-personalization, emotional intelligence, and seamless digital–physical experiences can redefine customer engagement. The chapter emphasizes feedback loops, ethical KPIs, and sustainability to ensure that AIoT deployments contribute to lasting value creation and corporate responsibility.

Chapter 8 analyzes emerging trends such as edge AI, federated learning, and quantum-IoT. It also discusses anticipated challenges like evolving cybersecurity threats, changing user expectations, and the increasing demand for ethical governance in autonomous systems.

The book concludes by synthesizing key insights and emphasizing the need for integrated sociotechnical thinking and human-centric strategies in AIoT deployment. Ultimately, the aim of this book is to serve as both a reference and a practical guide. It synthesizes lessons from technology, management, and ethics to provide a framework for deploying AIoT responsibly and effectively. By the end, readers will be equipped not only with technical and strategic knowledge but also with the human-centric mindset needed to shape AIoT ecosystems that are sustainable, inclusive, and ethically grounded.

On a personal note, this book reflects our conviction that the future of business transformation lies at the intersection of technology and humanity. Our own journey in this field has been shaped by conversations with practitioners, scholars, and leaders to whom we are grateful for their insights. We are deeply grateful to the editorial team at Springer Nature for their invaluable assistance throughout the publication process.

We hope this work encourages readers not just to adopt AIoT, but to do so in ways that strengthen trust, inclusivity, and long-term societal value.

Bengaluru, India	Surekha Borra
Kolkata, India	Nilanjan Dey
Taipei, Taiwan	Sheng-Lung Peng

Contents

1	**Introduction**	1
1.1	Origins of the Internet of Things (IoT)	1
1.2	Evolution of Artificial Intelligence (AI)	2
1.3	Emergence of the AIoT: Technological Convergence	2
1.4	Sociotechnical Implications and Awareness	3
2	**AIoT Landscape**	5
2.1	Architecture	5
2.2	Applications	7
2.3	Benefits	9
3	**AIoT Adoption and Challenges**	11
3.1	AIoT Adoption Strategy	11
3.2	Technical Challenges	14
3.3	Human-Centric Challenges in AIoT Adoption	15
3.4	Sociotechnical Readiness Factors	15
4	**Sociotechnical AIoT Deployment Framework**	19
4.1	Definition of Objectives	19
4.2	Assessment of Current Capabilities	20
4.3	Data Strategy	21
4.4	Cross-Functional Collaboration	22
4.5	Technology Selection	22
4.6	Skill Development	23
4.7	Risk Assessment	24
4.8	Regulatory Compliance	25
4.9	Ethical Considerations	25
4.10	Testing and Validation	26
4.11	Scalability and Flexibility	27
4.12	Monitoring and Maintenance	28
4.13	Feedback and Iteration	29
4.14	Sustainability	30
4.15	Human–System Interaction Design in the AIoT	31

5	**Governance Models and Change Management**	35
	5.1 Governance Models	35
	5.2 Governance Frameworks and Metrics	36
	5.3 Change Management Strategies	37
	5.4 Security and Privacy	39
6	**Human-Centric Design Practices in AIoT Systems**	43
	6.1 Human-Centred AI Principles	43
	6.2 Designing for User Trust and Transparency	44
	6.3 Inclusive and Accessible. AIoT Solutions	44
	6.4 Personalization Versus Privacy Trade-Off	45
	6.5 Cocreation and Participatory Design in the AIoT	45
7	**Human-Centric AIoT Strategies for Sustainable Business Evolution**	47
	7.1 AIoT and Hyperpersonalized Customer Experience	47
	7.2 Emotional Intelligence and Human-in-Loop Services	48
	7.3 Seamless Digital–Physical Convergence	49
	7.4 Continuous Learning Through Feedback Loops	51
	7.5 Strategic AIoT Alignment with Business Goals	52
	7.6 Ethical Value Creation Through Human-Focused KPIs	53
	7.6.1 Human-Centric KPIs	54
	7.6.2 Ethics-Driven ROI	54
	7.7 Strategic Sustainability for Long-Term Prosperity	55
	7.7.1 Long-Term Value Creation with AIoT	56
	7.7.2 Corporate Sustainability and the AIoT	56
8	**Evolving Challenges, Trends and Future Directions**	59
9	**Conclusions**	63

Appendix A: Glossary of Key Terms ... 65

Appendix B: AIoT Readiness Assessment Checklist ... 67

Appendix C: Examples of Human-Centric KPIs for AIoT Systems ... 69

Appendix D: Ethical AIoT Implementation Checklist ... 71

Appendix E: Regulatory Landscape ... 73

Appendix F: Tools and Platforms for AIoT Development ... 75

References ... 77

About the Authors

Surekha Borra (Senior Member, IEEE) earned her doctorate in image processing with a special focus on copyright protection of images from Jawaharlal Nehru Technological University, Hyderabad, India, in 2015. She started her academic career as an assistant professor in mid-2004 and served in various engineering colleges for 18 years. Currently, she is a professor in the Department of Computer Science and Engineering (IoT, Cybersecurity, and Blockchain Technology) at K. S. Institute of Technology, Bengaluru, India. Her research interests are image and video analytics, artificial intelligence, machine learning, biometrics, biomedical signal processing, and remote sensing. She has guided three research scholars and authored nine books and over 80 research articles in peer-reviewed journals and international conferences. Her international recognition includes services in various program committees and editorial and review boards, wherein she has been a guest editor for three journals and a reviewer for more than 25 refereed and indexed international journals.

She has received several research grants and awards from the Institution of Engineers (India) and the Karnataka State Government of India. She has received the Woman Achiever's Award from the Institution of Engineers (India) for her prominent research and innovative contribution(s), the Young Woman Achiever Award for her contribution to copyright protection of images, and the Distinguished Educator and Scholar Award for her contributions to teaching and scholarly activities.

Nilanjan Dey (Senior Member, IEEE) received the B.Tech., M.Tech. in information technology from West Bengal Board of Technical University and Ph.D. degrees in electronics and telecommunication engineering from Jadavpur University, Kolkata, India, in 2005, 2011, and 2015, respectively. Currently, he is professor with the Techno International New Town, Kolkata and a visiting fellow of the University of Reading, UK. He is the Editor-in-Chief of International Journal of Ambient Computing and Intelligence, Associate Editor of IEEE Transactions on Technology and Society and series Co-Editor of Springer Tracts in Nature-Inspired Computing and Data-Intensive Research from Springer Nature and Advances in Ubiquitous

Sensing Applications for Healthcare from Elsevier etc. Furthermore, he is an Editorial Board Member of IEEE Data Descriptions. He is a Fellow of IETE and member of IE, ISOC etc.

Sheng-Lung Peng is a professor and the director of the Department of Creative Technologies and Product Design, and the Dean of the College of Innovative Design and Management, National Taipei University of Business, Taiwan. He received the Ph.D. degree in computer science from the National Tsing Hua University, Taiwan. He is an honorary professor at Beijing Information Science and Technology University, China, and a visiting professor at Ningxia Institute of Science and Technology, China. He is also an adjunct Professor at National Dong Hwa University in Taiwan and Kazi Nazrul University in India. He is an Honorary Adjunct Professor in School of Management of Sir Padampat Singhania University and in School of Computer Science and School of Business of ITM (SLS) Baroda University, India. He serves as the president of the Association of Taiwan Computer Programming Contest and the Association of Algorithms and Computation Theory. He is a co-director of the ICPC Asia Pacific, and a director of the Institute of Information and Computing Machinery and the Taiwan Association of Cloud Computing. He is also a supervisor for the Chinese Information Literacy Association.

Dr. Peng has edited several special issues in journals, such as Journal of Internet Technology, IEEE Internet of Things Magazine, Computers and Electrical Engineering, Journal of Information Science and Engineering, and so on. His research interests are algorithm design in the fields of artificial intelligence, bioinformatics, combinatorics, data mining, and networking.

Chapter 1
Introduction

The twenty-first century has indeed seen an unprecedented acceleration of technological evolution marked by the merging of two highly transformative domains of our era: artificial intelligence and the Internet of Things. This joining of forces has led to the emergence of the artificial intelligence of things paradigm, where connected devices are capable not only of communicating and collecting data but also of thinking, learning and taking action independently. The artificial intelligence of things represents far more than mere technological fusion; it epitomizes a basic reorientation in how systems perceive, analyse and interact with their surrounding environment. Beyond devices that see and speak to one another, this novel innovation promises systems that observe the world on its own accord, draw inferences from what it witnesses and engages proactively with its setting.

1.1 Origins of the Internet of Things (IoT)

The concept of ubiquitous connectivity—connecting the digital and physical realms—is where the Internet of Things began. The first trials appeared in the 1980s, most notably with Carnegie Mellon University's well-known Coca-Cola vending machine, which was able to communicate its cooling and stock conditions over a network. The phrase "Internet of Things" was first used in 1999 by British technologist Kevin Ashton of MIT's Auto-ID Center to refer to a system in which the internet is connected to the physical world via ubiquitous sensors and data-sharing devices.

With the widespread use of sensors, RFID tags, embedded systems, and cloud computing in the 2000s, the Internet of Things rapidly expanded. The IoT created new service ecosystems and intelligent automation by making it possible to remotely operate physical things and record data in real time. Early IoT systems, however, were largely used as instruments for data collection and remote monitoring; they had no capacity to independently understand or act upon data.

© The Author(s), under exclusive license to Springer Nature Switzerland AG 2026
S. Borra et al., *AIoT Deployment in Business Evolution*,
SpringerBriefs in Computational Intelligence,
https://doi.org/10.1007/978-3-032-09472-8_1

1.2 Evolution of Artificial Intelligence (AI)

In the 1950s, the area of artificial intelligence was established with the goal of building robots that can carry out activities that normally require human intellect, such as language comprehension, learning, reasoning, and sensing. The creation of neural networks, expert systems, and symbolic logic systems was an early breakthrough. Even though there were periodic setbacks during the so-called AI winters, which were periods of decreased interest and financing, AI advanced steadily, particularly in the 1980s and 1990s, with the emergence of machine learning and statistical inference.

However, true innovation occurred in the 2010s with the introduction of deep learning, which was fuelled by advanced algorithmic models, large datasets, and greater computer power (such as GPUs). These advancements have allowed robots to surpass humans in a number of areas, including natural language processing, picture identification, and gaming.

1.3 Emergence of the AIoT: Technological Convergence

The combination of AI with the IoT, known as the AIoT, emerged in response to the limitations of the traditional IoT. While IoT devices can gather data, they lack the cognitive capacity to analyse and respond to it in real time. In contrast, AI systems require large quantities of data to train algorithms and models—data that IoT devices might provide. The AIoT paradigm supports edge intelligence, which means that data is not only gathered at the edge (for example, on devices or gateways) but also evaluated and processed locally via lightweight AI models. This minimizes latency, improves system autonomy, and ensures resilience in situations when cloud access is restricted or inconsistent.

The development of specialist AIoT chips, which integrates computing, sensing, and AI processing into a single low-power unit, allowing for decentralized decision-making at the device level, was a significant milestone in this convergence. AIoT therefore transforms the IoT from passive sensing to active, adaptive intelligence, in which devices not only monitor their surroundings but also learn from them and make context-aware judgments. This opens up significant opportunities across industries, including predictive maintenance in manufacturing, real-time traffic optimization in smart cities, energy-efficient buildings, precision agriculture, remote health diagnostics, etc.

1.4 Sociotechnical Implications and Awareness

The combination of artificial intelligence (AI) and the Internet of Things (IoT) has led to the emergence of a new field known as artificial intelligence of things (AIoT), which has the potential to enhance various aspects of daily life [1]. The current level of awareness and understanding of the AIoT among organizations and individuals varies significantly. According to a survey conducted by Gartner [2], by 2027, a quarter of global organizations are expected to be in the initial planning stages of incorporating AI. Simultaneously, 36% of organizations are anticipated to enter the experimentation phase, commencing the adoption of AI use cases characterized by significant business value but a comparatively low time-to-financial impact (TOFI). This forecast indicates a strategic shift in the AI landscape as organizations progressively transition from planning to experimentation.

According to a survey by PwC, Indian firms tend to adopt AI, with a 54% implementation rate [3]. Since IoT technology has been around for several years, there is a relatively high level of awareness of the technology among both organizations and individuals. According to the "State of IoT—Spring 2023" report by IoT Analytics [4], the global number of connected IoT devices is expected to reach 16.7 billion active endpoints. A study [5] indicated that IoT innovation has a prominent impact in Japan, Germany, and Australia, benefiting both society and businesses when its usage is customized to address identified problems. Furthermore, the study highlighted that the AIoT can be successfully deployed only on the existing infrastructure on which earlier technological advancements were made.

These surveys suggest that while there is a growing awareness of AI and IoT technologies among organizations, many are still in the early stages of adoption and have a limited understanding of hybrid technology's full potential. While the AIoT's technological trajectory is promising, its real-world implementation is influenced by social, organizational, and regulatory factors as well as by its technical capabilities. AIoT systems do not work in isolation; instead, they are entrenched in complex sociotechnical settings in which human values, institutional norms, ethical concerns, and political structures all play important roles in determining results. For example, an AIoT-powered smart grid might improve energy efficiency, but it also raises concerns about data privacy, algorithmic transparency, and labor effects. Wearable AIoT devices in healthcare can provide early warning signs of medical issues, but they may also raise concerns about personal health surveillance or data commodification. These instances highlight the need for a sociotechnical perspective, which balances technology capabilities with human-centered considerations.

To fully benefit from the AIoT, practitioners need increased education and awareness about AIoT challenges, sociotechnical readiness, security risks and measures, ethical use, and appropriate organizational adjustments.

The book delves into the technological, human, and organizational dimensions of deploying AIoT systems, highlighting the importance of sociotechnical readiness and human-centric approaches to ensure sustainable and ethical business transformation.

Chapter 2
AIoT Landscape

The AIoT, along with other hybrid technologies such as cloud, edge, and fog computing, increases the effectiveness of IoT applications [6] and has the potential to offer a variety of benefits in different sectors [7]. Those that successfully integrate the AIoT into their lives, businesses, and client service models stand to reap both short-term and long-term competitive advantages. However, it is important that individuals and organizations first comprehend the background of the AIoT and its architecture, applications, benefits and integration challenges.

2.1 Architecture

While AIoT is altering how humans interact with devices at home and at work, the result of this cutting-edge technology is a multiplication of data [8]. Significant amounts of bandwidth, availability, and power are needed to transport all the raw data back in real time to a private server or public cloud for processing or storage. In such cases, the migration of AI and machine learning to edge devices is highly recommended [9]. Although users must still train AI models in the cloud, by deploying trained AI models on edge devices, data gathering and inference may be carried out in the field [10]. The decentralized architecture of the AIoT in relation to cloud, fog, and edge computing with 3 core layers and 5 sublayers is shown in Fig. 2.1.

The bottommost and first layer is the perception layer, which comprises various long-range and short-range sensor nodes and devices. While the primary task of the sensing devices is to acquire ambient parameters [11], they also act as message transfer data mule nodes, most of which are associated with communication devices through communication networks such as Wi-Fi and Wi-Max, BLE, ZigBee, and LoRA. The edge-dew infrastructure of the network layer applies edge computing mechanisms to the aggregated data created in the perception layer on low-resource computation platforms. The dew buffer, which is another crucial component at this

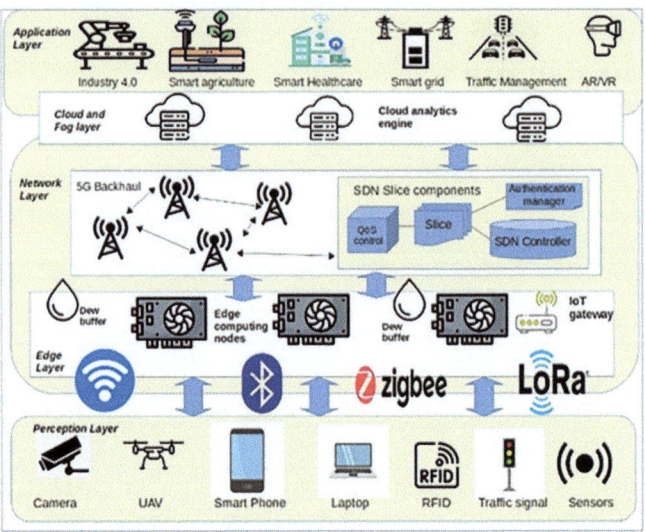

Fig. 2.1 Layered architecture of the AIoT

layer, has major significance for deploying dew as a service in an intermittently connected IoT network. In the case of real-time multimedia streaming, prefix catching is preferred over dew caching to ensure a lower round–trip delay. Another critical function of this layer is to divide the large-scale artificial intelligence component and assist the system in learning in a decentralized fashion. In this situation, the gateway is needed to provide communication between edge nodes and dew nodes, as well as low-latency connectivity between the fog and cloud architectures [12]. The primary communication element in the AIoT framework is the third layer, which consists of an ultralow-latency MIMO backhaul that primarily uses enhanced mobile broadband (EMBB), an enormous machine type of communication, for networking [13]. The integration of software-defined networks (SDNs) and network function virtualization (NFV) at this layer results in a high level of flexibility, agility, and scalability [14]. The network slicing theme employed at this layer enables the usage of slices of the resource that have been virtualized via software components, enabling efficient utilization of the network resources in an ultralow-latency network [15]. Finally, the capabilities of the application layer are utilized by all real-world applications that are connected primarily to users, such as healthcare, smart cities, Industry 4.0, and AR/VR. The actuation command can be sent directly from the cloud through the device to the cloud application or via the edge-dew-fog level.

In summary, with the help of all five sublayers, massive amounts of IoT sensor data, which are too large for cloud servers to handle in real time, are often transferred to network edge devices with the aid of fog and dew computing technologies. When the IoT sensors generate data, the AI at the edge analyses it to produce insightful information. In turn, the desired behaviour or action needed is sent as a command to the actuators in no time, thereby reducing latency, data transport, and storage costs. On the other hand, dew computing efficiently collaborates with cloud-based services while detaching apps from the cloud, enabling websites to be accessed even when there is no internet connection, increasing network availability, and enabling real-time decision-making and field action analytics that are efficient and productive.

2.2 Applications

Fully integrating AI and the IoT increases device accessibility and ensures that all collected datasets are utilized. Many industries, businesses, and households have already started using AIoT by employing linked machinery, end-user computers, appliances, personal gadgets, and other items while also adding a certain amount of intelligence [16]. This section briefly describes the disruptive applications of the AIoT and discusses how it influences contemporary civilizations. While there are several use cases for AIoT, the majority are aimed at automation, data management, downtime prevention, and operational efficiency. The AIoT uses machine learning algorithms to analyse video streams in real time and detect and identify objects, people, and activities [17]. Instead of requiring human operators to watch many video feeds, as is the case with traditional video management systems, AI and IoT integration make video surveillance smart. The use of the AIoT at retail shop check-in and check-out points aids in the detection of theft, intrusion, and firearms [18]. Amazon Go stores use IoT devices that automatically extract money from a customer's e-wallet in place of cashiers, streamlining the purchasing process to optimize the user journey.

The industrial sector is widely renowned for using the AIoT, which does not suffer from stress, exhaustion, or illness—three significant contributors to human errors in the workplace. Across all production units, the AIoT considerably increases the environmental awareness of smart manufacturing processes [19], which includes identifying trends, eliminating anomalous energy leaks, tracking energy peaks, looking for ways to reduce energy waste, and comprehending how each industrial asset influences total energy consumption [20]. AIoT also helps anticipate difficulties in avoiding expensive mistakes and worker hazards. Additionally, AI may assess ergonomics and suggest adjustments to help prevent repeated stress injuries or even worsening. The oil and gas industries, such as Shell, are utilizing AIoT and saving over a million dollars [21]. Critical real-time data representing oil flow, pressure, and temperature are captured by the IoT sensors deployed at their plants. They use AI to analyse data obtained from IoT sensors and pipeline monitoring systems in Nigerian oil fields and to suggest the ideal temperature and pressure to improve the process overall.

Real-time tracking of vehicles is made possible by a multitude of technologies, including cloud-based GPS, GPRS, RFID tags, and GIS, in addition to the AIoT. The data from the vehicle's fitted temperature, humidity, and fire sensors are supplied to the AI model on clouds in real time, which can spot irregularities and send out instantaneous alerts to stop any tragedy [22]. Today, the AIoT is utilized in fleet management to keep an eye on a fleet's cars, evaluate traffic patterns, design routes intelligently, identify risky driving practices, and monitor vehicle maintenance and delays [23]. Fuel expenses, time and expensive repairs can also be saved, as providers of automotive maintenance utilize real-time data gathered from sensors to anticipate failures and schedule repairs accordingly. Additionally, data analysis helps automobile makers find production flaws and fix them. Many other fields can benefit from the coexistence of the two technologies. Some clinical research firms have collaborated with analytics platforms to assess the impact of their medicines by subjecting real-time data collected from different sensors, wearables, and patients' mobile apps to machine learning and artificial intelligence analysis on the cloud [24]. This remote monitoring of real-time patient data avoids patients' frequent visits to clinics, apart from enhancing the patient experience and drug development. The cabin crews at smart airports can constantly monitor gate information updates, boarding queue activities, passenger positions, luggage monitoring, and other crucial activities in smart airports [25]. With microphones and connections, bank ATMs with NLP algorithms might hear the words "withdrawal" or "deposit" when a user speaks to them. By understanding the meaning of these words, the ATM is able to perform tasks appropriately, including accessing the correct page for the proper transaction [26].

Self-driving cars such as Tesla support hands-free driving, making driving safer, less stressful, and capable of making judgments that are similar to those made by humans because of the sophisticated IoT sensors, mounted cameras, powerful onboard computers, reliable software and hardware, and AI integration. A deep neural network model analyses the sensors' collected data in real time to determine what action the car should take next [27]. The weather and road conditions, other routes, best speed, and behavior of pedestrians under different situations may all be determined by self-driving automobiles.

Robotics and more sophisticated AI initiatives can work together to assist people. Given its basic ability to help people with disabilities and elderly individuals, the AIoT makes daily tasks easier and more pleasurable while also enhancing health [28]. Devices are programmed to operate and help people with cognitive and physical impairments [29]. Furthermore, APIs make it possible to provide battery-level information, describe app icons, and read messages for those who are blind or visually impaired. Facial recognition software enables wheelchair users to control their chairs via facial expressions. Users may also obtain information regarding wheelchair accessibility and wheelchair-accessible routes with voice or text guidance [30]. Elderly individuals or patients can also have their posture and signs monitored by AI, which has been integrated with non-invasive infrared thermal imagers in their bedrooms, bathrooms, or other private areas. If an abnormal temperature or fall is discovered in the monitored elderly, disabled, or patient, an alarm will sound, and a timely report will be sent to those in need of assistance. Automatically lighting doors and opening doors, playing genres that one enjoys, automatically adding and ordering provisions to the shopping list, and monitoring and lulling newborns to sleep are a few other applications. The basic potential of the AIoT in tracking fitness levels via wearables such as wireless earphones, AR/VR goggles, and smart watches is now enhanced

2.3 Benefits

to track yoga postures and sports strokes, heart rhythms, and heart failure via smart speakers, even without visiting personal trainers or doctors [31].

Smart farming, which includes IoT-based sensors, gathers temporal and geographical data, which they then send to a cloud server, where deep learning techniques comprehend the data, produce automated analysis, and identify patterns and forecasts, helping to increase the quality and quantity of agricultural products [32]. Intelligent pest management on farms tracks the population density of pests in potential hotspots via wireless image sensors mounted within greenhouses and in the surrounding environment [33].

In summary, the AIoT has been able to increase revenues while delivering greater value to customers of a wide range of industry verticals, including customized fitness, remote healthcare, precision agriculture, retail, autonomous cars, logistics, predictive maintenance, supply chains, oil and gas, manufacturing, industrial automation, banking, insurance, and services [34]. The devices became even more useful when combined with a sophisticated security infrastructure using AI.

2.3 Benefits

Companies have paired AI and IoT technologies for a variety of purposes, but principally to increase productivity and support new mobile and hybrid workplaces [35, 36]. In addition, for consumers who want to use it, the AIoT promises to provide several benefits [37–41], as listed in Fig. 2.2. The specific benefits of the AIoT shed light on how this integration enhances various aspects of technology and business.

Fig. 2.2 Benefits of AIoT

Chapter 3
AIoT Adoption and Challenges

AIoT's unique combination of artificial intelligence and the Internet of Things enables unprecedented levels of connectivity, automation, and data-driven insights. However, despite its promising potential, the successful adoption and scalability of AIoT are not solely determined by technological advancements. A comprehensive understanding of the sociotechnical ecosystem is essential to support its integration into real-world applications. This section explores AIoT adoption challenges and sociotechnical readiness factors for the effective deployment of the AIoT.

3.1 AIoT Adoption Strategy

A holistic approach for the adoption of the AIoT is composed of five phases, as shown in Fig. 3.1. This five-phase comprehensive strategy outlines an organization's commitment to the entire AIoT adoption journey, from inception to ongoing improvement and expansion.

Phase 1: Assessment and Planning: In Phase 1 of AIoT implementation, several critical steps lay the foundation for a successful adoption journey. First, it is essential to define clear business objectives and use cases, outlining the specific goals that the AIoT aims to achieve, whether it is optimizing operations, cutting costs, enhancing customer experiences, or exploring new revenue avenues. Prioritizing these use cases on the basis of their alignment with these objectives and potential return on investment is crucial. Next, thorough data assessment is imperative to understand the data landscape, which encompasses internal and external sources. This assessment delves into data availability, quality, and relevance, ensuring that the chosen use cases can be effectively supported by the available data. Simultaneously, technology evaluation is a pivotal aspect, where the existing IoT infrastructure, sensors, and devices are under scrutiny. This evaluation determines their compatibility with AI capabilities

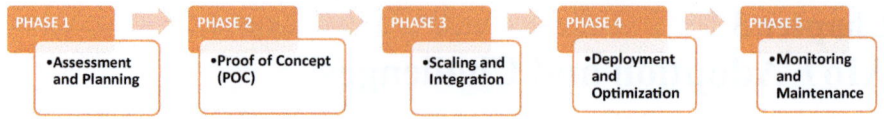

Fig. 3.1 AIoT adoption strategy in 5 phases

and assesses their ability to handle real-time data processing. Phase 1, therefore, serves as the groundwork for informed decision-making and sets the stage for a streamlined AIoT adoption process.

Phase 2: Proof of Concept (POC): This is a pivotal step in validating the technology's potential. In this phase, organizations carefully select a pilot use case, emphasizing both technical feasibility and strategic significance. The chosen use case should serve as a clear and compelling demonstration of the benefits that the AIoT can offer. Data collection and integration play a central role, involving the meticulous gathering and integration of data from diverse sources, such as IoT devices and sensors. Ensuring data quality and integrity is paramount for accurate analysis. Concurrently, model development takes shape with the creation of tailored machine learning models specific to the pilot use case. These models could encompass predictive maintenance algorithms, anomaly detection systems, or recommendation engines. The prototype implementation phase follows, wherein a functional AIoT system prototype is constructed, encompassing data processing, model deployment, and visualization components. This prototype offers a tangible representation of how the AIoT operates in a real-world scenario. Performance evaluation takes place in a controlled environment, involving rigorous testing of the prototype. Key performance indicators (KPIs) related to the use case are monitored, providing valuable insights into the effectiveness of AIoT technology. Additionally, feedback from end-users and stakeholders is gathered, ensuring that the POC aligns with expectations and requirements. Phase 2 thus serves as a crucial step in assessing the practical applicability of the AIoT and its potential to deliver tangible benefits.

Phase 3: Scaling and Integration: In Phase 3 of the AIoT adoption journey, scaling and integration take center stage as organizations prepare to expand the technology's footprint. The process begins with a thorough scalability assessment, wherein the requirements for scaling up the AIoT solution are determined. Factors such as data volume, device proliferation, and increased user demand are carefully considered to ensure that the system can handle growing needs. Infrastructure enhancement becomes a key priority, involving necessary upgrades to the IoT infrastructure. This might entail the adoption of cloud-based solutions for increased computing power and storage, leveraging edge computing for real-time processing, or improving connectivity to accommodate larger data flows. To fortify the AIoT ecosystem, organizations delve into data governance and security measures. Strengthening data governance practices becomes paramount to safeguarding data privacy and security. Robust measures, including access controls, encryption, and compliance protocols, are put in place to ensure the integrity and confidentiality of the data.

3.1 AIoT Adoption Strategy

Integration with existing systems is another critical aspect, as AIoT systems need to seamlessly mesh with existing IT and operational systems such as enterprise resource planning (ERP), customer relationship management (CRM), and data warehouses. This integration ensures smooth data flow and interoperability across the organization, enabling the AIoT solution to function harmoniously within the broader technological landscape. Phase 3 represents a pivotal stage in the AIoT adoption process, where scalability and integration efforts prepare the organization for the full realization of the AIoT's potential.

Phase 4: **Deployment and Optimization**: In Phase 4, deployment and optimization, organizations take their AIoT solution from the testing and scaling phases to achieve full-fledged production. The process begins with the full deployment of the AIoT solution, starting with a pilot use case that has been thoroughly tested and validated. Throughout this phase, diligent monitoring of system performance becomes crucial, enabling organizations to identify and promptly resolve any issues that may arise in a real-world operational environment. Continuous improvement is a core principle in Phase 4. Organizations recognize the need to refine and enhance their AI models continually. This involves the regular updating of models on the basis of new data and insights, as well as the optimization of algorithms for improved performance. By embracing a culture of continuous improvement, organizations ensure that their AIoT systems remain agile and responsive to changing needs. User training and adoption are also paramount during this phase. Providing comprehensive training to users and relevant teams ensures that they can effectively utilize the AIoT system's capabilities. This training not only empowers users but also fosters a culture of data-driven decision-making, where insights from the AIoT solution become integral to the organization's operations. Phase 4 marks the culmination of the AIoT adoption journey, where the organization realizes the full potential of its AIoT solution through effective deployment, optimization, and user engagement.

Phase 5: Monitoring and maintenance: In Phase 5, monitoring and maintenance, the focus shifts to ongoing care and optimization of the AIoT system. Performance monitoring becomes a continuous activity, with organizations diligently observing the system's performance and key performance indicators (KPIs). Proactive measures are taken to set up alerts for anomalies or system failures, enabling swift responses to potential issues. Regular updates are essential to ensure that the AIoT system is robust and secure. This involves a commitment to keeping AI models, software, and hardware up to date and applying necessary patches and upgrades to maintain both security and functionality. A vital aspect of Phase 5 is the establishment of a feedback loop with end-users and stakeholders. This feedback mechanism enables organizations to gather valuable insights and suggestions for improvement directly from those who interact with the AIoT system. This user-centric approach is integral to the system's evolution. Furthermore, Phase 5 encourages expansion and iteration. Building on the success of the initial use case, organizations actively seek opportunities to expand AIoT applications to other areas of the organization. This iterative approach ensures that the AIoT system remains aligned with evolving business needs and continues to deliver value.

This five-phase adoption strategy underscores the importance of aligning AIoT initiatives with overarching business goals and emphasizes the need for sustained monitoring and optimization. The generalized AIoT adoption strategy promises to revolutionize industries, enabling advanced automation, intelligent decision-making, and predictive maintenance. However, the successful adoption of the AIoT requires more than just technological advancements. A critical factor that plays a significant role is the sociotechnical readiness that influences AIoT adoption and implementation.

3.2 Technical Challenges

The AIoT is a complex and rapidly developing field with unique sociotechnical challenges that must be overcome to achieve successful adoption and implementation. One of the primary challenges is during the learning and training phase, where AI optimizes outcomes in AIoT systems. However, it might be difficult to predict whether the outcomes of subsequent iterations will be accurate. Owing to its impermanence, AI necessitates regular audits to maintain its reliability [42]. Another significant challenge is the amount of unbiased ground truth data needed for an AI model to represent a potential range of outcomes [43]. The availability of open-access datasets in many fields with correct data labelling and standardization is challenging [44]. Furthermore, since there is currently no single methodology, tool, or set of standard metrics for measuring and evaluating the performance of AI, user trust in the AIoT is limited [45]. While people's participation and information exchange are frequently essential to the success of AIoT projects, organizations' actions to increase the public's understanding of digital advancements are challenging. Understanding major AI and IoT concepts and evaluating how to apply them to everyday artefacts in real-world applications are explored.

In addition to data challenges, the governance and protection of data flows need to be addressed and controlled through monitoring and visibility tools. Many firms frequently lack the essential assurance of security until a problem arises, which can result in a variety of losses, including the loss of crucial data. Breaches that expose highly private information might have a negative influence on people's and organizations' privacy [46]. Therefore, it is critical to guard against unauthorized access to sensitive data while still providing essential and permitted access to the created data. Clear data management guidelines must be implemented to address privacy and security issues and to increase trust.

3.3 Human-Centric Challenges in AIoT Adoption

While AIoT adoption has enormous potential for operational efficiency and innovation, its implementation is frequently hampered by human-centric issues rooted in corporate psychology, workforce dynamics, and cultural views.

Resistance to change: Resistance to change is a recurring issue in digital transformation attempts. Employees may see AIoT as a threat to their jobs or autonomy, fearing a loss of control, authority, or relevance. This is especially true in conventional industries, where technology change may upend long-standing routines and hierarchies. Failing to address psychological resistance is one of the leading causes of failure in change programs. To create trust and minimize uncertainty, leaders must implement change management tactics on the basis of early communication, empathy, and participatory decision-making.

Fear of automation and job displacement: AIoT increases autonomy and decision-making capabilities at the edge, raising concerns about job displacement. Blue-collar workers and white-collar workers equally may see automation as a zero-sum game in which increased machine intelligence diminishes human employment. According to a World Economic Forum study (2023), while AI-driven technologies may displace specific occupations, they also present potential for employment augmentation, highlighting the importance of reskilling rather than replacement. To reframe the AIoT as a partner rather than a competition, organizations must actively convey the transition and build learning paths.

Mismatches in Skills and Capabilities: AIoT adoption frequently surpasses the workforce's current level of digital competency. The technical, administrative, and analytical skills needed to enable intelligent systems are becoming increasingly out of step with the capabilities found in many firms. Human–machine interaction design, data ethics, edge AI programming, and AI model interpretability are among the often undeveloped skills. This disparity will only grow in the absence of focused investments in reskilling and upskilling, which will negatively impact morale and productivity.

3.4 Sociotechnical Readiness Factors

Identifying and analysing the factors that influence the sociotechnical readiness of AIoT systems is critical for organizations and stakeholders aiming to deploy these technologies effectively. These factors encompass a wide range of considerations, including data management, organizational alignment, legal frameworks, and the sociocultural context in which AIoT solutions operate. By understanding these factors, decision-makers can better navigate the complexities of AIoT adoption, mitigate potential risks, and maximize the benefits of this transformative technology. The list of identified sociotechnical readiness factors includes the following:

- *Technology Readiness*: This refers to the availability and maturity of the technological infrastructure necessary for AIoT, including hardware, software, and communication systems. This factor also includes the level of technical expertise needed to design, deploy, and maintain AIoT systems [42, 43, 45, 48, 50, 52–59].
- *Data Management*: This refers to the management and governance of data generated by AIoT systems. This factor includes considerations such as data ownership, data privacy, and data security, as well as the use of advanced analytics and machine learning algorithms to extract insights from the data [49, 51].
- *Regulations and Standards*: These refer to the legal and regulatory frameworks that govern the use of AIoT systems, including privacy, security, and data protection laws. This factor also includes industry-specific standards and guidelines that govern the design, deployment, and operation of AIoT systems [64–66].
- *Business Strategy*: This refers to the alignment of the AIoT with organizational goals and objectives. This factor includes considerations such as the potential for cost savings, revenue generation, and competitive advantage using AIoT [60, 61].
- *Environmental Factors*: These factors refer to the physical environment in which AIoT solutions are deployed, such as the availability of infrastructure, network connectivity, and power supply, which can impact their adoption [62].
- *Sociocultural Factors*: These factors refer to the social and cultural norms and values that influence the adoption of AIoT systems. This factor includes considerations such as trust in AIoT systems, cultural attitudes toward automation and technology, and concerns about job displacement [44, 46, 47, 63–66].
- *Social Acceptance*: Social acceptance refers to the willingness of users to adopt and use AIoT systems. This factor includes considerations such as ease of use, the user experience, and the perceived value of the AIoT system to the user [5, 67].

Analysing the readiness levels of AI, the IoT, and the AIoT helps identify specific areas requiring improvement to ensure smooth implementation and scalability. Figure 3.2 illustrates the varying levels of readiness for AI, IoT, and AIoT technologies. Each technology has a unique set of strengths and challenges, with key factors such as technical infrastructure, data governance, regulatory compliance, and social acceptance playing pivotal roles in the adoption process. Despite AI exhibiting a high level of technical infrastructure readiness, it faces obstacles in terms of data governance, regulatory compliance, skill sets, business models, and social acceptance. Similarly, the IoT boasts high readiness for certain factors, such as technical infrastructure and skill sets, but it faces challenges in terms of data governance and social acceptance.

In contrast, the AIoT demonstrates an exceptionally high level of readiness across most factors due to the amalgamation of AI and IoT technologies. Nevertheless, it encounters hurdles in terms of data governance, regulatory frameworks, and social acceptance. All three technologies demand a robust technical infrastructure, necessitating potent hardware and software to process and analyse extensive data for AI, as well as network development and communication protocols for the IoT. Additionally, AI and the IoT, along with the AIoT, necessitate policies ensuring

3.4 Sociotechnical Readiness Factors

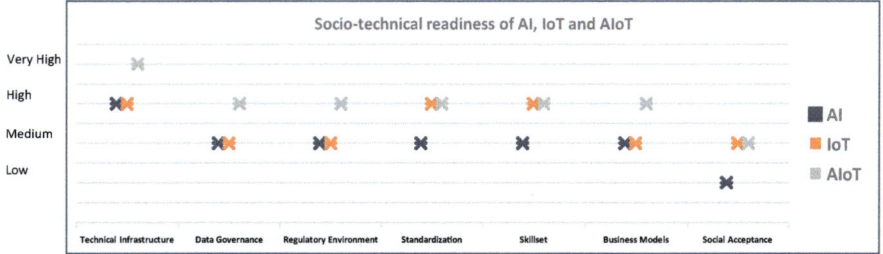

Fig. 3.2 Comparison of the sociotechnical readiness of the AI, IoT and AIoT

data privacy, security, and ethical usage, whereas the AIoT specifically requires governance frameworks addressing data from both realms.

Chapter 4
Sociotechnical AIoT Deployment Framework

Achieving sociotechnical readiness for the integration of the AIoT is an ongoing and multifaceted process. It necessitates a comprehensive approach that encompasses technological, human, and procedural dimensions. This readiness involves the meticulous preparation of both the technical infrastructure and the sociocultural aspects of AIoT implementation. This section proposes a comprehensive framework for the implementation and management of the AIoT with respect to sociotechnical readiness. Figure 4.1 shows that the framework is divided into four key phases: planning, execution, governance and compliance, and optimization and maintenance. Each phase contains critical activities that contribute to the successful deployment and ongoing management of AIoT systems.

The planning phase sets the foundation by defining objectives, assessing current capabilities, and establishing a data strategy. The execution phase involves the selection of appropriate technologies, fostering cross-functional collaboration, and developing the necessary skills. The Governance and Compliance phase ensures that ethical considerations, regulatory standards, and risk management are integrated into the process. The optimization and maintenance phase focuses on feedback loops, continuous validation, scalability, sustainability, and long-term system monitoring. Each component of the four phases is explained as follows.

4.1 Definition of Objectives

Establishing clear objectives is essential for sociotechnical readiness in AIoT adoption. This step aligns AIoT projects with both technical and organizational goals, ensuring their integration with broader business strategies. It involves identifying key challenges through in-depth analysis of root causes and aligning stakeholders with a common purpose. By addressing both technical feasibility and social impact, well-defined objectives ensure that AIoT solutions are focused, purposeful, and

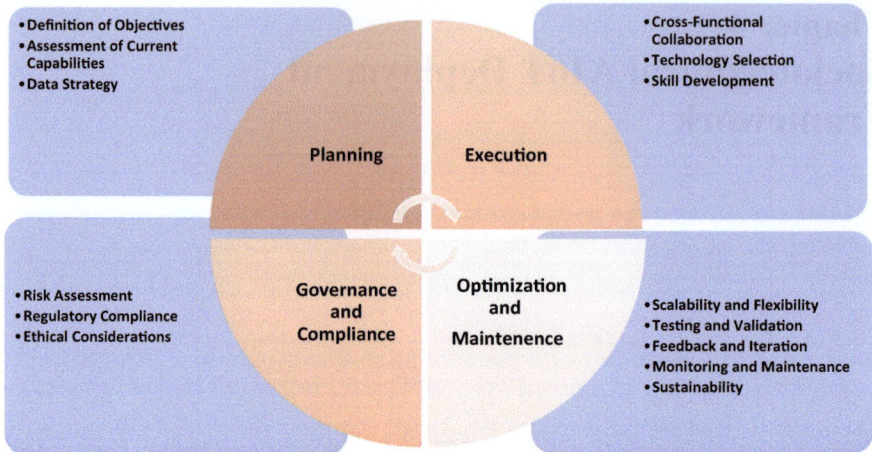

Fig. 4.1 Framework for comprehensive AIoT implementation and management

deliver real-world organizational benefits. A crucial part of this readiness is the in-depth analysis of specific issues to be addressed by AIoT technologies. It involves a thorough exploration of the root causes of organizational challenges, with a focus on identifying inefficiencies, pain points, or opportunities for enhancement. This analytical approach ensures that AIoT solutions are developed to address real-world, human-centric problems, supporting sociotechnical sustainability. Moreover, achieving sociotechnical readiness means aligning all stakeholders, from technical teams to end-users, and ensuring that resources are directed towards a common purpose. The definition of objectives must, therefore, incorporate both the technical feasibility and the socio-organizational impacts of the AIoT project. Ultimately, this step fosters direction, focus, and a shared vision, ensuring that the AIoT solution is not only technically sound but also socially aligned to deliver tangible, long-term benefits to the organization.

4.2 Assessment of Current Capabilities

A crucial step in achieving sociotechnical readiness for AIoT integration is assessing the organization's current capabilities. This assessment evaluates both technological and social aspects to ensure seamless adoption of AIoT solutions. It begins with a comprehensive review of the existing infrastructure, including hardware, software, and networking systems, to identify any gaps that may hinder AIoT integration. The focus is on scalability, compatibility, and readiness to support AIoT applications.

In addition to technology, sociotechnical readiness also emphasizes understanding how existing IoT devices and sensors align with operational needs. Creating an inventory of devices, examining their capabilities, and ensuring that they can effectively capture the necessary data for AIoT are critical steps.

Furthermore, the network architecture is evaluated not only for its technical capacity—such as bandwidth and latency—but also for its ability to support increased data flow and ensure robust security. By combining these technical evaluations with an understanding of organizational readiness, this step fosters a holistic approach, ensuring that both the technological infrastructure and the social systems are prepared for AIoT integration.

4.3 Data Strategy

A robust data strategy is fundamental to sociotechnical readiness for AIoT deployment, ensuring both technological and organizational alignment in managing and utilizing data. This strategy outlines how data will be collected, processed, stored, secured, and used to support the organization's goals, balancing technical needs with social and regulatory considerations. The strategy begins by identifying data sources within the AIoT ecosystem, such as IoT devices, sensors, customer interactions, and external providers. It considers structured, semistructured, and unstructured data types and the volume, frequency, and rate of data generation, which are crucial for effective integration with organizational processes.

Sociotechnical readiness highlights the importance of stakeholder collaboration, ensuring that decisions on data processing, whether real-time or batch, and the use of AI and machine learning algorithms reflect organizational needs. The strategy must also address where data processing occurs—whether at the edge of devices or in the cloud—ensuring technological and operational scalability. Equally important are data storage solutions that consider scalability, cost, and access speed, which are aligned with the organization's capacity to manage large datasets. The strategy includes data retention policies, ensuring compliance with regulations such as the GDPR and CCPA, and promoting data privacy and security measures, such as role-based access and encryption.

The sociotechnical dimension is reinforced through data governance, assigning roles for data ownership, stewardship, and ensuring data quality. It also emphasizes interoperability to enable seamless data flow across the organization. The strategy includes lifecycle management—backup, recovery, and archiving—and addresses data monetization opportunities. Ultimately, the data strategy must be well documented and communicated across all levels, fostering a shared understanding of the strategic value of data.

4.4 Cross-Functional Collaboration

Fostering cross-functional collaboration is essential for achieving sociotechnical readiness for AIoT adoption. Seamless teamwork among IT teams, data scientists, domain experts, and business leaders ensures that AIoT solutions are aligned with both technical requirements and broader organizational goals. This collaboration bridges the gap between technological capabilities and social and operational contexts, ensuring successful implementation. The key to fostering transparency, trust, and timely decision-making is effective communication across the following teams:

- IT teams play a crucial role in managing the technical infrastructure, including IoT devices, networks, and data storage, while also ensuring that cybersecurity measures are taken to protect AIoT systems. Their collaboration with other stakeholders guarantees smooth integration and continuous data flow.
- Data scientists have expertise in analysing IoT data through AI models, developing algorithms that extract valuable insights. Their collaboration with IT teams improves data quality and aligns AI models with business objectives, ensuring that AIoT solutions are both technically sound and socially relevant.
- Domain experts contribute deep industry knowledge, help define AIoT objectives, identify use cases, and validate AI-driven outcomes against real-world applications. Their involvement ensures that AIoT initiatives meet industry standards and respond to practical customer needs.
- Business leaders ensure that AIoT projects align with organizational strategies and secure resources, budgets, and executive support. Their involvement addresses risk management and ensures that AIoT initiatives are compliant with regulatory and business requirements.

In summary, cross-functional collaboration is not only a best practice but also a critical success factor in sociotechnical readiness for the AIoT. It fosters innovation, efficiency, and alignment with business objectives, ensuring that AIoT initiatives are both technically robust and socially integrated.

4.5 Technology Selection

The selection of appropriate AI and IoT technologies is a critical step in ensuring sociotechnical readiness for AIoT adoption. This process involves aligning technology choices with both organizational objectives and the sociotechnical context, ensuring that the selected technologies not only meet technical requirements but also integrate effectively within the broader social and operational systems. Scalability is a key factor, as the chosen technologies must accommodate future growth in IoT devices, data volume, and user demand without compromising performance. Sociotechnical readiness also requires that these technologies are compatible with existing IT infrastructure, ensuring smooth integration with current hardware, software, and data systems to avoid operational disruptions.

Security considerations are paramount in this decision-making process, especially when dealing with sensitive or personal data generated by IoT devices. The selected AI and IoT technologies must include robust encryption, access control, and authentication mechanisms to protect data throughout their lifecycle. The ability of AI technologies to process real-time data streams generated by IoT devices is also crucial. This requires evaluating the data processing, machine learning, and analytics capabilities of both AI and IoT technologies to ensure that they align with the organization's operational needs.

The decision between edge computing and cloud computing is another vital consideration. A hybrid approach may be beneficial depending on specific AIoT use cases, balancing performance and efficiency. In addition, the support ecosystem surrounding the chosen technologies, including community support, documentation, and vendor assistance, contributes to overall sociotechnical readiness by enabling smoother adoption and ongoing support. A comprehensive cost analysis is also necessary to factor both initial and operational expenses and evaluate the potential return on investment (ROI) in relation to AIoT objectives. Prototyping and testing the selected technologies in a controlled environment are recommended to validate their compatibility, scalability, security, and performance.

Finally, flexibility and adaptability are key to ensuring that the chosen technologies can accommodate evolving AIoT requirements and future enhancements. This sociotechnical approach ensures that technology decisions are not made in isolation but consider broader organizational and social contexts, ultimately driving the success of AIoT initiatives.

4.6 Skill Development

Investment in workforce skill development is essential for achieving sociotechnical readiness for AIoT adoption. Equipping employees with the necessary skills to leverage AI and IoT technologies ensures that the organization's technological advancements are supported by a socially and operationally prepared workforce. Skill development focuses not only on technical proficiency but also on aligning human capabilities with the evolving AIoT landscape. It enables employees to innovate, enhance efficiency, mitigate risks, and increase morale, contributing to both individual growth and organizational success. A sociotechnical approach to skill development recognizes the need to bridge the gap between technology and human expertise, ensuring that employees are active participants in AIoT integration. To implement this effectively, organizations should conduct skill gap analyses to understand the workforce's current capabilities and customize training programs to meet specific needs. This includes tapping into external training resources and fostering internal expertise to build a robust knowledge base. Cross-functional training also plays a key role, promoting collaboration across different teams and ensuring that employees understand both the technical and operational aspects of the AIoT. Training should cover key areas such as AI and machine learning, IoT device management, data security, analytics, and ethical AI practices, which are critical for aligning technological advancements with organizational values and ethical standards. Organizations should also measure progress through assessment metrics and ROI evaluations to ensure that training investments contribute to AIoT success. Ongoing support and inclusive access to training opportunities further enhance sociotechnical readiness, fostering a culture of continuous learning and adaptability.

4.7 Risk Assessment

Risk assessment is a pivotal recommendation for achieving sociotechnical readiness in the adoption of AIoT solutions. The intricate interplay between artificial intelligence and the Internet of Things presents unique challenges and uncertainties that organizations must effectively navigate. A comprehensive risk assessment process helps organizations identify, evaluate, and mitigate potential risks associated with AIoT adoption. First, risk assessment involves identifying various types of risks that can arise during AIoT deployment. These risks encompass technical challenges such as data security breaches, system failures, and algorithmic biases. Additionally, they extend to nontechnical risks, including regulatory compliance issues, privacy concerns, and ethical dilemmas. By categorizing these risks, organizations gain a clearer understanding of the multifaceted nature of AIoT adoption.

Once risks are identified, the next step is to assess their potential impact and likelihood. Organizations must evaluate the consequences of different types of risk for their AIoT initiatives, considering factors such as financial implications, reputational damage, and operational disruptions. Simultaneously, assessing the likelihood of each risk occurring helps prioritize mitigation efforts. High-impact, high-likelihood risks demand immediate attention, whereas low-impact, low-likelihood risks may receive less immediate focus. Mitigation strategies are an integral part of risk assessment. Organizations should develop and implement risk mitigation plans tailored to the specific risks identified. These strategies may involve enhancing data security measures, refining algorithmic models, or establishing robust incident response protocols. Additionally, organizations should proactively address ethical and compliance concerns by aligning their AIoT systems with relevant regulations and ethical frameworks.

Risk assessment is an ongoing process that should be revisited regularly to adapt to changing circumstances. As AIoT technologies evolve and new risks emerge, organizations must remain vigilant and update their risk mitigation strategies accordingly. Effective risk management involves continuous monitoring, testing, and refinement to ensure that AIoT deployments remain resilient and compliant with evolving standards and best practices.

4.8 Regulatory Compliance

Regulatory compliance is a critical component of sociotechnical readiness in AIoT adoption, ensuring that AIoT solutions are ethically, legally, and socially responsible. In a landscape where AI and IoT technologies evolve rapidly, organizations must navigate complex regulations, standards, and legal frameworks to ensure that their deployments not only achieve their goals but also adhere to societal expectations.

Compliance with existing regulations is essential, and depending on the AIoT application, this may involve adhering to data privacy laws such as the GDPR for general data protection or the HIPAA for healthcare-related applications. Ensuring compliance with such regulations builds trust with customers and stakeholders, safeguarding privacy and security while mitigating legal risk.

Proactively monitoring and adapting to emerging regulations and standards is equally important. As new laws and guidelines specific to AI and IoT technologies are introduced, organizations must remain updated to maintain compliance. This often requires dedicated compliance teams or officers who ensure that AIoT solutions remain aligned with legal frameworks. Transparency plays a vital role in regulatory compliance, fostering accountability and trust. Organizations should maintain clear documentation of their AIoT processes, data usage, and decision-making algorithms, which not only aids in regulatory audits but also reassures users about how their data are being handled. Appointing a data protection officer (DPO) or compliance officer may be necessary to oversee adherence to legal requirements, manage data protection impact assessments, and communicate with regulatory bodies when needed.

In addition to data privacy, regulatory compliance also extends to cybersecurity standards, product safety regulations, and ethical guidelines. Comprehensive risk assessments help organizations identify potential compliance gaps and develop strategies to address them, ensuring that their AIoT solutions are both secure and legally compliant. By prioritizing compliance, organizations not only meet legal and ethical obligations but also build trust with stakeholders, protect sensitive data, and position themselves for sustainable success in the AIoT era.

4.9 Ethical Considerations

Ethical considerations constitute a cornerstone of sociotechnical readiness in AIoT adoption, ensuring the responsible and ethical use of technology that aligns with societal values. The development of ethical guidelines for AIoT deployment addresses critical issues such as bias mitigation, transparency, accountability, and data privacy, integrating both the technical and social dimensions into the decision-making process. To mitigate bias, organizations must recognize its potential in AIoT systems and proactively address it by refining training data and algorithms. This promotes fairness and inclusivity in AI-driven decisions. Transparency is essential and is achieved through explainable AI, clear algorithm documentation, and open communication with stakeholders, ensuring that AIoT systems are understandable and accessible. Accountability is reinforced by defining clear roles for data governance and algorithm management. The formation of interdisciplinary ethics committees, involving diverse perspectives from technology, business, and ethics, ensures a balanced approach to AIoT deployment. Data privacy is a critical concern, with a focus on embedding privacy protections, implementing consent mechanisms, and regularly evaluating the ethical implications of each AIoT use case.

Engaging stakeholders in discussions around ethics and providing ongoing education and training for employees fosters a culture of responsibility. Continuous monitoring of ethical considerations is vital, allowing organizations to adapt as new ethical challenges emerge and technologies evolve. Prioritizing ethics within the AIoT framework not only builds trust among stakeholders but also ensures that AIoT technologies align with broader social values. This sociotechnical approach ensures that AIoT solutions serve both organizational goals and the public good, contributing to sustainable, responsible innovation and society.

4.10 Testing and Validation

Testing and validation are critical components in achieving sociotechnical readiness for AIoT adoption. In complex and interconnected AIoT ecosystems, these processes ensure the reliability, safety, and sociotechnical alignment of systems. Comprehensive testing is the first step, starting with functional testing to ensure that AI algorithms and IoT devices perform their tasks as intended. This involves evaluating diverse use cases and scenarios to identify flaws early, reducing the risk of operational or user disruptions. Performance testing follows, where the system's scalability and efficiency under varying loads, network conditions, and environmental factors are assessed. This step is crucial to ensure that the AIoT infrastructure can handle increasing data volumes and user demands. Security testing is essential because of the vulnerability of AIoT systems to cyber threats. By conducting penetration testing and vulnerability assessments, organizations can protect sensitive data and maintain user trust. Equally important is interoperability testing, which ensures smooth communication and data exchange between diverse devices and algorithms within AIoT environments.

A sociotechnical approach to testing also requires ethical scrutiny. AIoT systems must be assessed for potential biases or unintended discriminatory effects, particularly when sensitive data are handled or critical decisions are made. Testing should ensure fairness and transparency across all AI and IoT components. Validation complements testing by confirming that AIoT systems meet predefined objectives and align with ethical standards. This includes user acceptance testing, where feedback from real users ensures that the system is effective, usable, and beneficial. The incorporation of user perspectives strengthens the alignment between technology and organizational goals.

Given the evolving nature of the AIoT, continuous testing and validation are vital. As systems are updated, organizations must maintain ongoing monitoring to identify new issues and adapt to both technological and ethical developments. In summary, thorough testing and validation processes are essential for sociotechnical readiness, ensuring that AIoT systems function reliably, securely, and ethically. This proactive approach builds user trust, strengthens system performance, and aligns AIoT deployments with both technical and social standards.

4.11 Scalability and Flexibility

Scalability is essential in the context of AIoT systems, which often involve numerous IoT devices generating vast amounts of data. To achieve sociotechnical readiness, organizations must design their AIoT infrastructure to accommodate increasing data traffic, device proliferation, and evolving user demands without compromising performance. Scalability in this context means that systems can efficiently manage the growing complexity of AI algorithms and data processing. This readiness is crucial not only for handling larger volumes of data but also for supporting more sophisticated AI models that require greater computational resources as they evolve. Ensuring scalable AIoT solutions empowers organizations to meet changing user needs and market conditions effectively.

Flexibility complements scalability by allowing organizations to adapt to unforeseen challenges and capitalize on new opportunities. AIoT systems must be designed to integrate new IoT devices, data sources, or AI algorithms easily, ensuring that organizations can pivot quickly in response to changing business conditions. Flexibility fosters interoperability, a key aspect of sociotechnical systems, by enabling diverse devices and technologies from different vendors to work together seamlessly. Embracing standardized interfaces and protocols ensures smooth interactions across a broad ecosystem, enhancing the adaptability of AIoT deployment. Additionally, flexibility allows the customization of AIoT systems to suit specific industry needs, ensuring that the technology aligns with distinct use cases and regulatory requirements. This ability to tailor solutions to industry-specific ethical guidelines or regulatory standards enhances both technical and social alignment, making the system more valuable and compliant.

By prioritizing scalability and flexibility, organizations position themselves for long-term success, ensuring that their AIoT deployments are adaptable, efficient, and socially responsible.

4.12 Monitoring and Maintenance

Monitoring in the context of AIoT involves real-time surveillance and assessment of data flows, system performance, and the behavior of AI algorithms. To achieve sociotechnical readiness, organizations must implement robust monitoring tools and procedures that allow them to proactively identify anomalies, technical glitches, security threats, and deviations from expected operational standards. Early detection through comprehensive monitoring minimizes system downtime and safeguards the reliability of AIoT systems. Moreover, monitoring ensures alignment with both technical and societal expectations, as it provides a mechanism to assess how well the system is meeting user needs and responding to broader ethical or regulatory concerns.

Maintenance complements monitoring by focusing on the ongoing upkeep, updates, and optimization of AIoT systems. This involves regular updates to both software and hardware components, ensuring that they stay aligned with industry standards, security protocols, and business objectives. Regular maintenance also addresses evolving security threats, vulnerabilities, and the need to optimize AI algorithms for changing environments. Keeping AI models up-to-date and refining their performance is key to sustaining sociotechnical readiness, as it ensures that the system continues to meet both technical benchmarks and societal goals, such as fairness, transparency, and privacy.

A critical aspect of monitoring and maintenance is the collection and analysis of performance data. Organizations must track system metrics, user interactions, and the outcomes of AI models to assess their effectiveness and identify opportunities for improvement. This data-driven approach informs decisions related to algorithm optimization, resource allocation, and system enhancements, ensuring that AIoT deployments remain efficient, secure, and adaptable to both technical and social changes. Additionally, these practices should extend to data management and governance. Given that data form the foundation of AIoT systems, ensuring data integrity, quality, and privacy is paramount. Regular audits, data cleansing, and strict adherence to data privacy regulations, such as the GDPR or HIPAA, are essential for maintaining trust and compliance. These efforts demonstrate a commitment to both technical performance and societal responsibility.

Cross-functional collaboration plays a crucial role in monitoring and maintenance. IT teams, data scientists, and domain experts must work together to interpret data, identify areas for improvement, and develop strategies for ongoing optimization. This collaborative approach ensures that AIoT systems are continually refined in response to technical advancements and societal expectations.

4.13 Feedback and Iteration

Feedback mechanisms play a pivotal role in gathering insights from a diverse array of stakeholders, including end-users, data scientists, domain experts, and IT teams. These stakeholders provide valuable perspectives on the performance, usability, and relevance of AIoT solutions. Actively collecting feedback at various stages of the AIoT adoption process allows organizations to identify strengths, weaknesses, and areas for improvement, fostering a culture of collaboration and shared responsibility.

User feedback is particularly important, offering insights into how well AIoT systems meet user expectations and needs. Organizations should prioritize soliciting and listening to user input to identify pain points, usability issues, and feature requests. This focus on user-centric design helps drive iterative improvements that enhance the overall user experience, ensuring that AIoT solutions are not only technically sound but also socially relevant and accessible. In addition to user input, feedback from data scientists and domain experts is critical for refining AI models and algorithms. These experts can help identify biases, improve data quality, and optimize algorithms to generate more accurate and actionable insights from IoT-generated data. Fostering open communication and collaboration between technical teams and domain-specific experts is essential for leveraging feedback effectively and ensuring that AIoT solutions address real-world challenges.

Iteration represents the process of making continuous updates and enhancements on the basis of the feedback received. This involves refining AI algorithms, improving data processing pipelines, and optimizing system performance. An iterative approach enables organizations to respond proactively to changing circumstances, emerging technologies, and evolving business requirements. Moreover, iteration is closely linked to the principles of agile development, where AIoT solutions are developed and deployed incrementally. This agile methodology promotes flexibility and responsiveness, enabling organizations to deliver value to users more quickly while adapting to shifting priorities and minimizing risks associated with large-scale, monolithic deployments.

Establishing feedback loops within the organization is crucial for integrating insights gained from feedback into the decision-making process. Regular meetings, reviews, and retrospectives create opportunities for teams to reflect on feedback and make data-driven decisions regarding system improvements. This cycle of reflection and adaptation fosters a culture of continuous learning and collaboration, strengthening the sociotechnical readiness of AIoT deployments.

4.14 Sustainability

Sustainability is a pivotal recommendation for achieving sociotechnical readiness in AIoT adoption. This holistic approach encompasses environmental impact, scalability, lifecycle management, energy efficiency, responsible data management, regulatory compliance, social responsibility, and continuous improvement. A sustainable approach ensures that AIoT technologies contribute positively to both business objectives and the well-being of society and the planet.

Environmental sustainability involves designing AIoT systems that minimize energy consumption, reduce waste, and limit the carbon footprint. Organizations should prioritize the use of energy-efficient IoT devices, optimize data processing algorithms to reduce computational demands, and explore renewable energy sources for powering their infrastructure. By adopting environmentally friendly practices, organizations can not only comply with regulatory standards but also appeal to environmentally conscious consumers and stakeholders.

Social sustainability emphasizes the importance of equitable access to AIoT technologies. Organizations must ensure that their solutions are designed with inclusivity in mind, enabling diverse populations to benefit from AIoT innovations. This involves considering the varying needs of different user groups and ensuring that technology is accessible to all, regardless of socioeconomic status. Engaging with community stakeholders during the design and deployment phases fosters a sense of ownership and accountability, ensuring that AIoT solutions are not only effective but also socially responsible.

Economic sustainability requires organizations to implement business models that support long-term viability while balancing profitability with social and environmental responsibility. This involves exploring innovative approaches such as circular economy principles, where products are designed for reuse, recycling, or refurbishment, minimizing waste and extending the lifecycle of devices. Moreover, sustainable business practices help build trust and credibility with customers and investors, enhancing brand loyalty and reputation. A critical aspect of promoting sustainability in AIoT deployments is collaboration across disciplines and sectors. Engaging cross-functional teams, including IT professionals, environmental specialists, social scientists, and business leaders, ensures that diverse perspectives are considered in decision-making processes. This collaborative approach enhances the ability to identify and mitigate potential risks associated with sustainability, ensuring that AIoT initiatives are aligned with both technical and societal goals.

Monitoring and evaluating sustainability metrics are also essential for assessing the impact of AIoT systems on environmental and social dimensions. Organizations should establish key performance indicators (KPIs) that measure energy usage, waste reduction, user engagement, and social outcomes. Regularly assessing these metrics enables organizations to make informed decisions, adapt strategies, and continuously improve the sustainability of their AIoT solutions.

In conclusion, sustainability is a foundational recommendation for achieving sociotechnical readiness in AIoT adoption. By prioritizing environmental, social,

4.15 Human–System Interaction Design in the AIoT

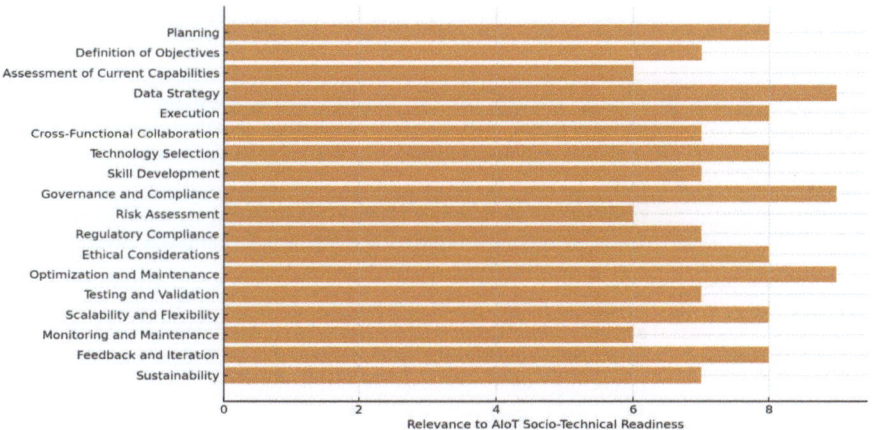

Fig. 4.2 Relevance of components to AIoT sociotechnical readiness

and economic sustainability, organizations can ensure that their AIoT systems not only deliver technical advantages but also contribute positively to the broader community and the environment. Embracing sustainability as a core principle fosters trust, drives innovation, and positions organizations for long-term success in the evolving landscape of AIoT technologies.

Each component of the proposed AIoT implementation framework discussed in this section not only contributes to the technical success of the system but also ensures its alignment with human, organizational, and societal needs, as shown in Fig. 4.2. The bar chart in Fig. 4.2 visually represents the relevance of each component to AIoT sociotechnical readiness. The chart highlights how various components rank in importance when AIoT implementation is considered. The relevance is measured on a scale of 10. Table 4.1 summarizes how each component of the proposed AIoT framework discussed is related to sociotechnical readiness.

4.15 Human–System Interaction Design in the AIoT

Successful AIoT implementation is dependent on the quality of human–system interaction—the interface between intelligent machines and their human users. Unlike typical automation systems, AIoT apps make judgments, learn from user behavior, and frequently function partially autonomously. This complicates interaction and necessitates the design of systems that are intuitive, explainable, and trustworthy.

Human–system interactions must be built via principles from the human-centered design (HCD) and user experience (UX) methods. Interfaces should be visible (explainable AI), sensitive to user feedback, and adaptive to different degrees of technical knowledge. For example, healthcare practitioners utilizing AIoT for patient

Table 4.1 Sociotechnical readiness relevance to the components of the proposed AIoT framework

Planning	
Definition of objectives	Involves aligning AIoT goals with social needs, business objectives, and stakeholder expectations. This ensures that the system's purpose resonates with users and society, fostering acceptance and engagement
Assessment of current capabilities	Evaluates not only technical infrastructure but also organizational readiness, skills, and cultural fit. By considering both technical and social environments, it helps avoid potential conflicts between the system and its users
Data strategy	Considers the technical management of data (e.g., storage, security) and social implications (e.g., data privacy, ethical usage). A balanced data strategy ensures the system meets technical requirements while respecting users' rights and societal norms
Execution	
Cross-functional collaboration	Encourages collaboration between technical teams and social scientists, ethicists, and other stakeholders. This ensures the AIoT system is designed with diverse perspectives, leading to better integration into sociotechnical contexts
Technology selection	Involves choosing technologies that are not only efficient but also align with user skills, organizational processes, and societal standards. The right technology will enhance user acceptance and reduce friction between technical capabilities and human usability
Skill development	Focuses on equipping both technical personnel and users with the necessary skills to interact with the AIoT system. Building technical skills while addressing social training needs ensures smooth adoption and minimizes resistance
Governance and compliance	
Risk assessment	Involves identifying both technical risks (e.g., system failure) and social risks (e.g., user mistrust or privacy concerns). A thorough risk assessment helps in designing safeguards that address the sociotechnical landscape comprehensively
Regulatory compliance	Addresses legal and regulatory frameworks that govern both the technical deployment and its social impact. By ensuring compliance, the system avoids legal challenges and societal pushback, enhancing readiness for widespread adoption
Ethical considerations	Ensures that the system adheres to societal values and ethical standards, making it more acceptable to users and reducing concerns over misuse or unintended harm. This helps build trust, which is crucial for sociotechnical readiness
Optimization and maintenance	
Testing and validation	Includes testing for technical functionality and user acceptance. Ensuring that the system works as intended from both perspectives improves its sociotechnical readiness, as it minimizes frustration and ensures reliability

(continued)

Table 4.1 (continued)

Optimization and maintenance	
Scalability and flexibility	Ensures the system can grow technically (e.g., adding more devices) while also adapting to social changes (e.g., new regulations or shifts in user behavior). A flexible system is better equipped to thrive in dynamic sociotechnical environments
Monitoring and maintenance	Continuous monitoring of both system performance and social acceptance helps identify and resolve issues quickly. Proactive maintenance that considers user feedback ensures ongoing sociotechnical harmony
Feedback and iteration	Collects feedback from both technical performance metrics and user experiences. This ensures the system evolves in a way that addresses technical issues while also adapting to changing social expectations and user needs
Sustainability	Addresses both technical sustainability (e.g., energy efficiency) and social sustainability (e.g., long-term user satisfaction and societal benefits). A sustainable system ensures long-term sociotechnical integration, as it aligns with broader social goals like environmental responsibility and ethical AI usage

monitoring should not require extensive technical understanding, but they should comprehend the reasoning behind system suggestions.

Chapter 5
Governance Models and Change Management

Effective governance is critical to the effective deployment and operation of artificial intelligence of things (AIoT) systems. This ensures that these systems are aligned with business goals, meet legal standards, and handle ethical concerns. This section examines several governance models for AIoT ecosystems, such as centralized, decentralized, and federated methods, as well as the importance of public–private partnerships, governance tools and indicators, and change management strategies.

5.1 Governance Models

Governance models for AIoT systems can be broadly categorized into centralized and decentralized frameworks, each with distinct characteristics, advantages, and challenges. In a centralized governance model, a single authoritative body is in charge of all decision-making, policy creation, and enforcement inside the firm. This strategy provides policy and process consistency, allowing for constant compliance and efficient administration. However, it may result in bottlenecks, decreased flexibility, and delayed responses to local situations.

In contrast, a decentralized governance model distributes decision-making authority among the organization's divisions or units. This strategy provides greater flexibility and response to local circumstances, but it may cause inconsistencies and difficulties in maintaining overall compliance and standards. The decision between centralized and decentralized governance models is determined by aspects such as organizational structure, size, and the complexity of AIoT installations. Some companies may use a hybrid approach, using components from both models to strike a balance between control and flexibility.

The federated governance model strikes a balance between centralized and decentralized systems. It combines centralized oversight with decentralized execution, allowing individual units to function independently within a framework of overarching norms and standards established by a central authority.

Public–private collaboration AIoT initiatives frequently involve partnerships between public and commercial institutions and the use of shared resources, skills, and infrastructure. These collaborations can spur innovation and enable large-scale deployments. However, such collaborations must manage hurdles such as harmonizing varied goals, ensuring fair data sharing, and resolving concerns about public interest and privacy.

5.2 Governance Frameworks and Metrics

The implementation of strong governance demands the use of tools and metrics to track compliance, performance and effect. Frameworks such as COBIT (Control Objectives for Information and Related Technologies) and ISO/IEC 38500 offer systematic guidelines for IT governance that may be tailored to AIoT situations. COBIT is an IT governance framework developed to oversee and manage enterprise IT. It enables enterprises to integrate IT with business objectives, optimize the value of IT expenditures, and efficiently manage IT resources. ISO/IEC 38500 is the worldwide standard for information technology corporate governance, and it includes concepts, definitions, and a model to assist directors in understanding its necessity. It establishes six principles: assign duties, plan to best serve the business, make purchases for solid reasons, ensure essential levels of performance, ensure rule compliance, and maintain respect for human elements.

The key measures for assessing AIoT governance may include the following:

- *Compliance Rate*: The compliance rate refers to the percentage of AIoT devices, systems, and components that adhere to established regulations, industry standards, and governance policies. In the context of AIoT governance, this metric is critical for ensuring that smart devices and AI algorithms operate within ethical, legal, and technical boundaries. These regulations may cover areas such as data privacy, cybersecurity, device interoperability, and environmental impact. A high compliance rate indicates strong regulatory alignment and responsible innovation, whereas a low compliance rate could signal risks, such as data breaches, algorithmic bias, or safety hazards.
- *Incident Response Time*: Incident response time measures the duration between the identification of an AIoT-related issue (such as a data leak, malfunction, or ethical breach) and the resolution or mitigation of that issue by the responsible authorities. Timely response is crucial in AIoT ecosystems because of the interconnected nature of devices and the real-time impact of potential threats. A fast response reduces the potential for cascading failure, reputational damage, or harm

5.3 Change Management Strategies

Table 5.1 AIoT governance metrics

Metrics	Example	Use case
Compliance rate	An AI-powered surveillance camera following GDPR guidelines on data collection and storage	Regular audits and certification processes can be implemented to monitor compliance across AIoT networks
Incident response time	A city's smart traffic system encounters a software bug; the response time measures how quickly engineers fix and redeploy the corrected firmware	Deployment of automated alert systems and emergency protocols to enhance response capabilities
Stakeholder satisfaction	Consumer feedback on data transparency in wearable health devices, or developer input on the clarity of AI regulatory guidelines	Incorporating stakeholder input into policy revisions to ensure alignment with evolving technological and societal expectations

to users. This metric helps evaluate the agility, preparedness, and effectiveness of governance frameworks.

- *Stakeholder Satisfaction*: Stakeholder satisfaction gauges the perceived effectiveness, fairness, and transparency of AIoT governance mechanisms from the perspective of various stakeholders, including developers, users, regulators, and citizens. Governance is not just about rules and enforcement; it is also about building trust and maintaining collaborative relationships. This metric involves collecting qualitative and quantitative feedback through surveys, interviews, or performance evaluations. High satisfaction indicates that governance frameworks are not only functional but also respected and inclusive.

Regular assessment via the metrics listed in Table 5.1 ensures that governance structures remain effective and responsive to evolving challenges. Furthermore, selecting and implementing an appropriate governance model is vital for the successful deployment of AIoT systems. Organizations must carefully consider their specific needs, regulatory environment, and operational complexity to choose a model that ensures compliance, promotes innovation, and aligns with strategic objectives.

5.3 Change Management Strategies

AIoT adoption frequently causes not only technical disruption but also significant emotional and cultural shifts within enterprises. Effective change management must handle these "soft" components as well as the strategic and structural elements. Emotional Responses to Technological Change.

Employees may experience a range of emotions, including exhilaration, worry, skepticism, and even anger. These emotions might be triggered by a sense of loss of control, dread of the unknown, or a lack of faith in one's capacity to adapt. Even if the technology foundation is strong, emotional reluctance can subtly hamper execution. Leaders must take an emotionally intelligent approach, acknowledging and accepting these emotions while providing psychological safety, mentorship, and clear paths to upskilling.

Another important consideration is the cultural compatibility of AIoT technology with existing company values. For example, in highly centralized settings, the flexible, data-driven attitude necessary for AIoT may conflict with traditional command-and-control systems. In contrast, cultures that value innovation and learning are more likely to adopt AIoT as a growth facilitator.

Cultural change activities must be intentional, including value rearticulation, incentive realignment, and narratives that connect AIoT adoption to the organization's vision and purpose. Change agents should promote the story of "collaboration with technology" rather than "conquest by technology."

To successfully integrate AIoT technologies and ensure sociotechnical readiness, organizations must prioritize key change management strategies. These strategies focus on fostering an adaptive, innovative, and well-prepared environment, which can be achieved through the following essential measures:

- *Cultural Shift*: Change management fosters a cultural transformation within the organization, creating an environment that encourages innovation, adaptability, and continuous learning. These attributes are essential for embracing AIoT technologies effectively. By promoting a culture that values experimentation and open-mindedness, organizations can prepare their workforce to adapt to new processes and technologies with enthusiasm.
- *Skill Development and Training*: Ensuring that employees are not only aware of the benefits of AIoT but also equipped with the necessary skills is fundamental. Tailored training programs should be designed to address the specific needs of various roles within the organization. This proactive approach enables employees to feel confident in the use of AIoT technologies, reducing the anxiety associated with change.
- *Leadership Support*: Strong leadership is paramount in change management. Leaders must champion AIoT initiatives and clearly communicate a strategic vision that articulates the benefits and implications of AIoT adoption. When leaders actively support the transition, they help build trust and encourage buy-in from employees.
- *Stakeholder Engagement*: Involving diverse stakeholders—including IT teams, data scientists, domain experts, and business leaders—is central to a successful change management strategy. Engaging these groups ensures that various perspectives are considered, addresses concerns, and facilitates collaboration. This holistic approach enhances the collective understanding of the potential impact of the AIoT on organizations.
- *Effective Communication*: Open and transparent communication is crucial to ensure that all stakeholders are informed about the progress of AIoT initiatives. By regularly updating employees on changes and outcomes, organizations can mitigate the resistance and uncertainty associated with the transition.

- *Empowerment of Change Champions*: Identifying and empowering change champions within an organization can significantly accelerate the adoption of AIoT solutions. These individuals act as advocates for the initiative, helping motivate their peers and fostering a supportive atmosphere for change.
- *Constructive Management of Resistance*: Change management recognizes that resistance is a natural response to change. By implementing techniques to identify and address resistance, organizations can create a more supportive environment. This may involve offering additional training or involving employees in decision-making processes to foster ownership of the changes.
- *Pilot Projects and Iterative Implementation*: Conducting pilot projects before full-scale AIoT implementation allows organizations to test concepts and gather valuable insights. Change management facilitates the planning and execution of these projects, enabling organizations to refine their strategies on the basis of real-world experiences.
- *Ongoing Monitoring and Feedback*: Change management is not a one-time effort; it requires continuous monitoring and the establishment of feedback loops to make iterative improvements. This adaptive approach ensures that AIoT initiatives remain aligned with the organization's goals and address emerging challenges.
- *Risk Mitigation and Sustainability*: Integral to change management are strategies for risk mitigation, including the development of contingency plans. Ensuring that AIoT initiatives are sustainable in the long term reinforces the commitment to a successful transition.

In summary, change management is essential for effectively managing the human aspects of AIoT adoption. By fostering a culture of innovation and adaptability, promoting skill development, engaging stakeholders, and implementing strategic communication, organizations can enhance their sociotechnical readiness. This comprehensive approach prepares the workforce to embrace AIoT technologies, ultimately driving transformative change and achieving organizational success in the evolving digital landscape.

5.4 Security and Privacy

AIoT success is not only about smart systems but also about building trusted, respectful relationships between technology and its human stakeholders. Given the ubiquitous nature of AIoT devices, which continually gather data from personal surroundings, privacy by design is not only a best practice but also a must. The principle of privacy by design advocates embedding privacy measures into technology architectures from the outset rather than retrofitting protections after deployment. To ensure AIoT security, data reduction, decentralized processing, anonymization, and clear user permission frameworks should be considered. Transparent communication regarding data usage and user rights is critical for building confidence.

AIoT systems rely significantly on real-time and historical data; therefore, ethical data management is critical to their responsible usage. This extends beyond compliance with rules such as the General Data Protection Regulation (GDPR) and the California Consumer Privacy Act (CCPA). It calls for a principled approach to concerns such as data ownership, algorithmic transparency, and equal access to benefits.

The cybersecurity measures encompass stringent access controls, the encryption of data in transit and at rest, the deployment of firewalls and intrusion detection systems for monitoring network traffic, and regular software updates to ensure that the latest security patches are applied. Vulnerability assessments and penetration testing are regularly conducted to identify and promptly address weaknesses in AIoT systems, with the added benefit of threat intelligence informing proactive defense measures. A comprehensive incident response plan is developed, ensuring that all stakeholders are well versed and trained in the plan's execution.

Data privacy compliance involves meticulous adherence to the GDPR, particularly when the personal data of EU citizens are processed, with requirements spanning explicit consent for data processing, data subject rights enforcement, and mandated breach notifications to authorities. Similarly, compliance with the HIPAA is essential when handling healthcare data, necessitating robust safeguards for protected health information (PHI).

Furthermore, adopting data minimization practices, incorporating privacy considerations from the outset of AIoT system design, securing user consent, and ensuring transparency in data usage are essential tenets. Respecting data subjects' rights and providing mechanisms to address their requests are integral components.

Efforts to increase security awareness and training, involving regular employee education on cybersecurity best practices and data privacy regulations, are crucial. Evaluating the cybersecurity practices of third-party vendors and suppliers contributing to the AIoT solution is equally important for ensuring alignment with security and privacy standards.

The incorporation of secure coding practices during AIoT software and application development, coupled with routine code reviews, helps identify and mitigate security vulnerabilities before deployment. Continuous monitoring through security audits, vulnerability assessments, and penetration testing aids in the identification and remediation of security weaknesses, whereas incident response drills serve to increase the efficacy of response plans.

Some specific and customized recommendations for AIoT environments for safeguarding data privacy and security necessitate proactive and multifaceted strategies as follows:

- *Edge-Based Encryption*: Implement encryption mechanisms at the edge, where data are generated, to protect it during transmission. Lightweight cryptographic algorithms suitable for resource-constrained IoT devices are used.
- *Differential Privacy*: Differential privacy techniques are applied to aggregate and analyse data while preserving individual privacy. This allows for useful insights without exposing sensitive information.

5.4 Security and Privacy

- *Federated Learning*: Employ federated learning, where AI models are trained on local devices without centralizing data. This minimizes the exposure of raw data to central servers.
- *Homomorphic Encryption*: This method explores homomorphic encryption, which enables computations on encrypted data without decryption. This can be valuable for AIoT applications that require data analysis while preserving privacy.
- *Local Anonymization*: Anonymize data at the source by removing personally identifiable information or using techniques such as k-anonymity and l-diversity.
- *Secure Device Authentication*: Implement strong device authentication protocols to ensure that only authorized devices can interact with the AIoT system, reducing the risk of unauthorized access.
- *Secure Boot and Firmware Updates*: Enabling secure boot processes and mechanisms for secure firmware updates to protect IoT devices from malicious tampering.
- *Blockchain for Data Provenance*: Leveraging blockchain technology to create an immutable ledger of data transactions, ensuring data integrity and traceability.
- *AI-Enhanced Intrusion Detection*: AI can be utilized for real-time intrusion detection and anomaly detection within AIoT systems to promptly identify security threats.
- *Secure Model Deployment*: Robust security measures, including model encryption, signature verification, and containerization, are applied when AI models are deployed at the edge.
- *Behavioral Analysis*: Behavioral analysis algorithms are implemented to detect unusual device or user behavior patterns, which could indicate security breaches.
- *Privacy Impact Assessments*: Privacy impact assessments are conducted to identify potential privacy risks and develop strategies to mitigate them throughout the AIoT system lifecycle.
- *User Consent and Control*: Give users greater control over their data by providing clear consent options and mechanisms to revoke access or delete their data from AIoT systems.
- *Third-Party Audits*: Engage third-party security auditors to assess the privacy and security of AIoT systems periodically, ensuring compliance with best practices and standards.
- *Regulatory Compliance*: Staying informed about evolving privacy and security regulations specific to AIoT and ensuring full compliance in all aspects of system development and deployment.
- *Secure Supply Chain*: Ensure the security of the entire supply chain, from device manufacturing to deployment, to prevent the introduction of vulnerabilities at any stage.
- *Incident Response Plan*: Develop a comprehensive incident response plan that outlines steps to take in the event of a security breach, including data breach notification procedures.
- *User Education*: Educate end-users about the importance of privacy and security in AIoT systems, promoting responsible use and behavior.

- *Redundancy and Failover*: Implement redundancy and failover mechanisms to ensure system availability in the face of security incidents or attacks.
- *Ethical AI Governance*: Establishing governance frameworks that address not only technical security but also ethical considerations, ensuring that AIoT systems uphold societal value.

These recommendations should be integrated into the design, development, and ongoing management of AIoT systems to create a robust privacy and security foundation while harnessing the benefits of AI and IoT integration.

Ultimately, the implementation of robust security measures and sustained adherence to data privacy regulations are ongoing and dynamic processes. As cyber threats continually evolve, organizations must remain agile and adapt their security strategies to address emerging challenges and vulnerabilities. By proactively addressing security and privacy concerns, organizations not only safeguard sensitive data and maintain the integrity of AIoT systems but also build trust with users, which is a critical aspect of AIoT success.

Chapter 6
Human-Centric Design Practices in AIoT Systems

The AIoT is a relatively new concept, and there is a limited understanding of its technology. As AIoT involves the integration of AI algorithms with diverse IoT devices and complex platforms, ensuring seamless integration while maintaining data flow and functionality becomes challenging. Ensuring that the vast amount of data generated by combining AI and the IoT is not only efficiently processed but also leveraged synergistically for meaningful insights and decision-making is another challenge. Organizations and individuals are investing in the research and development of best practices and innovative solutions to address the unique concerns and challenges in AIoT adoption. This section presents detailed case studies across various sectors, illustrating the transformative impact of the AIoT and the best practices that have emerged from these implementations.

The combination of artificial intelligence (AI) with the Internet of Things (IoT), also known as AIoT, is transforming business and society by allowing intelligent, context-aware systems. However, for these technologies to gain universal adoption and beneficial societal influence, they must be created with a strong human-centric focus. Human-centric AIoT design guarantees that intelligent systems complement rather than replace human skills, respect user autonomy, and are consistent with basic values such as trust, inclusion, and transparency. This section explores the essential aspects of humancentricity in AIoT development.

6.1 Human-Centred AI Principles

Human-centered AI puts people, not algorithms, at the heart of design, development, and deployment. According to Ben Shneiderman [68], human-centered AI must be dependable, safe, and trustworthy. It should empower people by improving their decision-making abilities rather than replacing them. In the context of the AIoT, which includes autonomous cars, healthcare devices, smart homes, and industrial automation, this notion entails developing systems that adapt to human goals while being under human control. A smart health monitoring system, for example, should notify users of abnormalities, propose actions, and allow them to analyse and regulate responses.

Global frameworks reflect this human-centered worldview. The OECD's AI Principles [69] and the European Commission's Ethics Guidelines for Trustworthy AI [70] both stress principles including justice, accountability, and openness. When these concepts are implemented in AIoT systems, they assure both technological functionality and social accountability. The actual goal is to operationalize these principles in complex, dispersed systems where decisions are made in both physical and digital contexts.

6.2 Designing for User Trust and Transparency

Trust is the foundation of every successful AIoT system. As these systems become more autonomous and engage with people in real time, establishing and maintaining trust becomes a technological and psychological requirement. Users must understand how AIoT systems function, why they act in the way they do, and what data are being used. This need for intelligibility motivates the creation of explainable AI (XAI), a field aimed at making algorithmic judgments understandable to nonexperts [71].

In practice, trust-building in the AIoT entails creating interfaces that provide transparency in data flows, decision logic, and system limits. For example, a smart home assistant should provide contextual information on how it learns user preferences in addition to responding to orders. Predictability and consistency in performance help to develop trust. Systems that demonstrate irregular behavior, even if technically better, might damage user trust. The communication of failure limits, ethical limitations, and backup processes is critical for creating a responsible and human-centered user experience.

6.3 Inclusive and Accessible. AIoT Solutions

Human-centeredness is inadequate without inclusion. AIoT systems must be developed to suit people of all ages, abilities, cultural origins, and socioeconomic statuses. The objective is not only to prevent exclusion but also to actively build equal and accessible settings. Inclusive AIoT design requires consideration of both physical accessibility, such as voice-enabled or tactile interfaces for people with impairments, and cognitive accessibility, such as simpler user experiences for those with minimal digital literacy. For example, smart city applications must examine how older people engage with AI-powered transportation systems, ensuring simplicity of use without the need for sophisticated interfaces. Furthermore, datasets used to train AIoT models must be representative to prevent systemic biases that may disadvantage underrepresented populations [72]. Accessibility includes cost and infrastructural issues. AIoT devices in low-resource environments must operate with minimum bandwidth, work offline when necessary, and provide localized language options. The truly inclusive AIoT sees diversity as a design benefit rather than a restriction.

6.4 Personalization Versus Privacy Trade-Off

Personalization is a highly valued characteristic of AIoT systems. Intelligent technologies that learn users' preferences, routines, and behaviors can provide personalized experiences ranging from energy-efficient smart homes to proactive healthcare notifications. However, this customization frequently comes at the expense of widespread data gathering and monitoring, resulting in complicated trade-offs between user comfort and privacy. In the age of surveillance capitalism, many AIoT technologies are based on commercial models that commodify personal information [73]. Users may experience ease while being oblivious of how their actions are tracked, profiled, and monetized. To solve this problem, designers must apply a "privacy by design" approach [74], which incorporates data reduction, permission processes, and user controls into the system architecture.

Personalization should be carried out with openness and respect for autonomy. Users must be able to opt out, change settings, or choose local data processing over cloud-based options. Ethical personalization necessitates a shift in both technological design and commercial ethics, with a focus not only on what the AIoT can accomplish but also on what it should do in the service of human dignity and freedom.

6.5 Cocreation and Participatory Design in the AIoT

Cocreation, or the active participation of stakeholders in the design and implementation of AIoT systems, is an important aspect of human centricity. Participatory design techniques use local knowledge, lived experiences, and contextual insights to guarantee that technologies are meaningful, useful, and morally appropriate. This technique is especially important in public-sector applications, such as smart urban infrastructure, because choices influence several populations and shared places. Cocreation goes beyond user testing and involves communities in the early stages of problem conceptualization and prototyping. For example, while building a smart mobility platform, planners can work with users from diverse demographic groups—cyclists, parents with strollers, and people with disabilities—to better understand real-world limits and goals. Such collaboration not only enhances system relevance but also fosters civic trust and a sense of ownership [75].

Participatory design also serves as a mechanism for identifying and addressing ethical blind spots. Diverse perspectives surface risks and unintended consequences that designers or engineers may overlook. In this sense, cocreation is not just a method but also an ethical commitment to democratizing innovation and ensuring that AIoT systems serve collective well-being.

Chapter 7
Human-Centric AIoT Strategies for Sustainable Business Evolution

In the era of AIoT, the customer experience (CX) has transformed into a dynamic, data-driven, and emotionally intelligent engagement model. Businesses are no longer simply service providers; they are experience curators. The combination of AI and IoT technology enables businesses to anticipate consumer demands, respond in real time, and create adaptive, customized experiences that span both digital and physical domains. However, as automation advances, preserving empathy, diversity, and trust becomes increasingly important.

On the other hand, to have long-term effects on AIoT systems, their implementation must be strategically integrated with overall corporate objectives and social duties. Strategic alignment ensures that AIoT investments are not only technically solid but also contextually meaningful, supporting both operational objectives and stakeholder preferences. Value realization in this setting is multifaceted and includes economic rewards, ethical performance, employee empowerment, and long-term viability.

This section looks at how the AIoT improves client experiences through hyperpersonalization, emotional intelligence, seamless integration, and iterative design. Furthermore, this section discusses how firms may align their AIoT strategy with their purpose, values, and consumer expectations and defines new success measures that reflect efficiency and empathy.

7.1 AIoT and Hyperpersonalized Customer Experience

The confluence of artificial intelligence (AI) with the Internet of Things (IoT), known as AIoT, is transforming how businesses perceive and connect with their consumers. AIoT systems provide hyperpersonalized customer journeys by recording, processing, and analysing data in real time, allowing organizations to provide contextually relevant experiences on the basis of individual preferences, behaviors, and requirements. Hyperpersonalization goes beyond standard personalization tactics by combining AI technologies, such as machine learning, natural language processing (NLP), and deep learning, with IoT-generated data streams to create dynamic consumer profiles. These profiles are constantly updated with information from smart devices, sensors, wearables, and mobile apps [76].

This real-time connection enables businesses to anticipate user intent, provide predictive suggestions, and engage customers at the most appropriate touchpoints [77]. For example, in retail, the AIoT allows firms to observe in-store consumer movements via smart cameras and RFID sensors and then correlate these observations with previous purchase history and online activity. This comprehensive data integration allows real-time suggestions, dynamic pricing, and targeted marketing [78]. In the automobile sector, connected vehicles equipped with AIoT solutions adjust infotainment systems, climate settings, and route suggestions depending on driver preferences and contextual data such as time of day or traffic circumstances [79]. Furthermore, the AIoT plays an important role in omnichannel consumer interaction plans. By syncing data from wearables, smart home devices, and smartphone engagements, businesses can provide a consistent and tailored experience across digital and physical platforms. AIoT data fusion generates a feedback loop that not only personalizes present encounters but also influences future product development and service upgrades [80].

However, developing hyperpersonalized experiences via the AIoT is not without hurdles. Key difficulties include protecting data privacy and security, enabling interoperability across diverse devices, and retaining user confidence in automated decision-making processes. To reduce these risks and enable the ethical deployment of AIoT solutions, organizations must include human-centric design principles as well as transparent data governance structures [81].

In essence, the combination of AI and the IoT allows for unparalleled degrees of customization in consumer experiences. As AIoT technologies evolve, strategic implementation becomes critical to developing customer-centric business models, deepening engagement, and maintaining a competitive edge in a quickly changing digital world.

7.2 Emotional Intelligence and Human-in-Loop Services

As AIoT technologies become more thoroughly integrated into customer-facing and operational processes, emotional intelligence (EI) and human-in-the-loop (HITL) mechanisms are widely acknowledged as critical for providing empathic, context-aware, and ethically sound service delivery. In this context, emotional intelligence is defined as the system's capacity to perceive, analyse, and respond to human emotions via data inputs such as voice tone, facial expressions, physiological signals, and language patterns [82]. AIoT devices equipped with affective computing capabilities, such as smart cameras, voice assistants, and biometric wearables, may detect emotional indicators in real time and adjust their replies or service suggestions appropriately.

This has significant implications in industries such as healthcare, elder care, education, and retail, where the emotional environment influences user engagement, satisfaction, and outcomes [83]. AIoT-enabled elder care systems, for example, can detect tiny changes in voice, facial tension, or movement as indicators of loneliness, anxiety, or cognitive impairment. These insights can warn caregivers or establish reassuring interactions via voice assistants via emotionally adaptable language [84]. Similarly, customer service bots with emotion recognition can escalate conversations to human agents when discomfort or discontent is detected, resulting in a more empathetic response [85].

This incorporation of human supervision, termed human-in-the-loop (HITL), is critical for ensuring ethical control, accountability, and transparency in AIoT systems. HITL frameworks guarantee that AI choices, particularly those with moral or emotional ramifications, are subjected to human assessment and intervention as needed [86]. This is especially essential in cases where the AI may misread emotional cues or act on inadequate information. Furthermore, HITL services make continuous learning for AI systems possible by combining human feedback with model training and fine-tuning. Such feedback loops improve AI systems' contextual sensitivity and emotional accuracy over time, resulting in more robust and human-centered solutions [87].

However, the effective implementation of emotionally intelligent AIoT systems and HITL services necessitates close attention to sociotechnical preparedness. Organizations must encourage multidisciplinary cooperation among engineers, behavioral scientists, and ethicists to create systems that are not only technically sound but also psychologically and socially suitable. Data privacy, emotional manipulation hazards, and algorithmic bias are all serious issues that must be addressed by open regulations, consent frameworks, and explainable AI architectures.

Finally, the combination of emotional intelligence and AIoT, together with human-in-the-loop processes, paves the way for systems that are not only intelligent but also emotionally sensitive and morally aligned. These characteristics are critical for building trust, empathy, and human-centeredness in the next generation of AIoT services.

7.3 Seamless Digital–Physical Convergence

The integration of digital and physical experiences marks a watershed moment in AIoT-enabled ecosystems. Seamless digital–physical convergence is the integration of physical environments with digitally enhanced services to create immersive, intelligent spaces that respond in real time to user behavior, environmental stimuli, and contextual information [88]. This convergence, facilitated by AIoT infrastructures, affects how organizations generate value, communicate with consumers, and improve operations in industries such as retail, manufacturing, smart homes, and urban infrastructure. At the heart of this convergence are AI-powered IoT devices that gather and analyse data from physical spaces—such as motion sensors, RFID tags, cameras, and environmental sensors—and utilize it to coordinate digital services and automated reactions. These systems may adjust lighting, temperature, product suggestions, and even spatial arrangements in response to real-time user interactions and preferences [89]. For example, in smart retail environments, AIoT technologies can use augmented reality (AR) overlays to guide consumers through the shop, measure product interaction, and trigger tailored promotions depending on the customer's location and behavior.

In manufacturing and logistics, convergence enables intelligent factories in which AI algorithms read sensor data from equipment and humans to optimize operations, predict maintenance requirements, and decrease downtime. These cyber-physical systems provide a feedback loop between digital twins, or virtual versions of physical systems, and their real-world counterparts, enabling predictive insights and ongoing improvement [90]. Similarly, AIoT-enabled smart cities use digital–physical convergence to control traffic flows, monitor public health, and deliver citizen-centric services via data-driven urban planning. One of the most disruptive characteristics of digital–physical convergence is its ability to dissolve conventional barriers between online and offline channels, allowing for real omnichannel experiences. Customers, for example, can start a product interaction in a virtual environment (e.g., a mobile app or a smart assistant), continue it in a physical store equipped with AIoT sensors, and finish the journey with an automated checkout or delivery system—all informed by a continuous data stream and contextual awareness [91].

Despite its potential, achieving seamless digital–physical convergence poses significant problems. These include interoperability across devices and platforms, delays in real-time decision making, and the requirement for strong cybersecurity standards to secure linked systems [92]. Furthermore, the design of such experiences must be based on human-centric concepts to avoid cognitive overload and enable intuitive interactions between users and settings. As a result, enterprises must invest not only in technological infrastructure but also in the sociotechnical preparedness of their teams and stakeholders. This involves encouraging cross-functional collaboration among engineers, designers, data scientists, and behavioral specialists to construct adaptable, ethical, and user-friendly settings.

To summarize, AIoT-driven digital–physical convergence is a pillar of the growing experience economy. Businesses may build more engaging, efficient, and customized experiences by embedding intelligence into settings and linking physical presence with digital capacity, resulting in a substantial shift toward ambient, anticipatory service ecosystems.

7.4 Continuous Learning Through Feedback Loops

One of the most important aspects of AIoT systems is their capacity to participate in continuous learning via feedback loops. This dynamic feature enables AI models to grow in real time in response to new data, interactions, and environmental changes, creating an environment in which systems not only adapt to but also anticipate human demands and behaviors. In AIoT ecosystems, feedback loops are critical for increasing system performance, customizing user experiences, and boosting decision-making accuracy in industries such as retail, healthcare, and manufacturing.

Feedback loops collect input from multiple touchpoints (sensors, user interactions, environmental conditions, and operational metrics) and utilize it to inform and change AI system behavior. For example, in retail, AIoT systems may observe consumer interactions, product preferences, and purchase habits in real time, allowing the system to refine product suggestions, optimize pricing strategies, and dynamically alter inventory management. This ongoing improvement results in more relevant and tailored experiences for users, enhancing consumer engagement and happiness.

In industrial applications, AIoT systems may monitor machinery performance via real-time sensor data and predictive analytics. When a sensor identifies an abnormality or anticipates an approaching failure, it initiates a feedback loop that activates maintenance schedules or modifies machine operations to avoid future problems. This feature decreases downtime, improves operational efficiency, and lowers maintenance costs, which are critical for sectors that rely on highly automated production systems. The notion of continuous learning via feedback loops is more than just enhancing the technical performance of AI systems; it also plays an important role in refining the human experience. For example, AI-powered virtual assistants, chatbots, and customer care bots may learn from each encounter, progressively improving their capacity to recognize subtleties in language, tone, and context. Over time, the system improves its ability to respond to complicated questions and emotional signals, resulting in more human-like and empathic interactions [93].

Furthermore, feedback loops in AIoT systems constitute an important mechanism for enabling human-in-the-loop (HITL) models, which include human knowledge in the decision-making process. Continuous input from human operators in HITL settings assists AI systems in correcting errors, refining forecasts, and making more accurate judgments, particularly in scenarios requiring ethical judgment or deep domain knowledge. This human–AI collaboration not only improves the accuracy of AI models but also ensures that AI systems adhere to human values and society standards.

However, implementing continuous learning through feedback loops poses various obstacles. These include worries about data privacy, the difficulty of incorporating input from diverse data sources, and the risk of algorithmic drift—when models become less accurate over time if they are not adequately monitored and changed. To reduce these dangers, firms must establish strong governance frameworks that include clear data usage regulations, safe data processing methodologies, and explainability in AI decision-making processes [94]. Furthermore, organizations must engage in the ongoing training of AI models, which necessitates committed resources and a long-term feedback management approach.

In conclusion, continuous learning via feedback loops is the cornerstone of adaptive, intelligent AIoT systems. AIoT systems may continually improve their performance, adapt to user requests, and maximize operational savings by incorporating real-time data and continuing feedback into their learning processes. This continual innovation enables organizations to remain competitive in fast-paced contexts while also creating richer, more personalized customer experiences.

7.5 Strategic AIoT Alignment with Business Goals

The effective deployment of AIoT systems necessitates more than just technological innovation; it also necessitates strategic alignment between AIoT efforts and larger corporate goals. Strategic alignment ensures that AIoT investments improve organizational performance, increase competitive advantage, and satisfy key performance indicators (KPIs) that are linked with a company's long-term objectives. This approach entails integrating AIoT capabilities with key business goals, processes, and value propositions to ensure that each AIoT solution meets a specific business need.

First, AIoT alignment requires a thorough grasp of the company's strategic vision and commercial objectives. Companies must determine how AIoT technologies may improve operational efficiency, customer engagement, innovation, and product development. For example, in the manufacturing industry, AIoT may be strategically used to improve production processes, monitor equipment health, and decrease waste, resulting in cost savings and increased productivity. AIoT-powered smart shelves and tailored customer experiences can help retailers increase sales, improve inventory management, and increase customer loyalty.

Furthermore, AIoT alignment necessitates a comprehensive approach to data strategy. As AIoT systems create massive volumes of data from connected devices and sensors, organizations must use these data to acquire actionable insights that can aid decision-making and performance monitoring. Data governance is a critical component of this approach, ensuring that data acquired from multiple sources are correct, safe, and in accordance with applicable legislation. Organizations with a strong data infrastructure may employ AIoT analytics to improve business strategies, manage operations, and provide tailored customer care.

AIoT alignment is also crucial for developing novel business models. Businesses may improve customer experiences and generate new income streams by incorporating AIoT technology into their goods or services. For example, in the automotive industry, connected vehicles equipped with AIoT systems provide not only improved user experiences (e.g., autonomous driving, real-time traffic updates) but also new business opportunities for service models such as pay-per-use and subscription-based services. Similarly, in healthcare, the AIoT supports the shift from reactive care models to proactive health management, with remote patient monitoring and predictive analytics leading to fewer hospital readmissions and better patient outcomes.

Strategic congruence with company objectives necessitates a strong leadership structure and organizational preparedness. The implementation of AIoT solutions must be supported by senior management and incorporated into the organizational culture. Leaders must create a collaborative atmosphere in which cross-functional teams from IT, operations, marketing, and customer support can effectively execute AIoT plans. This involves ensuring that appropriate technical and human resources are available to support AIoT activities and that the organization's culture welcomes digital transformation.

Furthermore, organizations must emphasize the scalability and adaptability of their AIoT systems to guarantee that they can adapt as business demands change. Strategic vision is essential to discover potential for developing AIoT use cases and incorporating future technologies such as 5G, blockchain, and edge computing. A future-proof AIoT strategy allows firms to remain adaptive in the face of technology breakthroughs and changing market dynamics, resulting in long-term value generation. However, attaining strategic alignment is not without problems. Overcoming legacy infrastructure limits, managing change opposition, and resolving data privacy and security issues are all significant challenges.

Finally, optimizing the value of AIoT investments requires strategic alignment with business goals. Companies may improve their operational efficiency, stimulate innovation, and achieve long-term success by incorporating AIoT technologies into their overall vision, data strategy, and business models. Strategic alignment guarantees that the AIoT is more than just a form of technological improvement but rather a critical facilitator of company transformation and competitive advantage in the digital era.

7.6 Ethical Value Creation Through Human-Focused KPIs

The incorporation of AIoT technologies into company plans involves a reconsideration of established performance indicators. While key performance indicators (KPIs) and return on investment (ROI) have long been the foundations of business evaluation, the rise of the AIoT has created a need for human-centric KPIs and ethics-driven ROI frameworks that are in sync with both technological advancements and societal expectations. These new KPIs prioritize providing value for not only the business but also its stakeholders, such as customers, workers, and the larger community, ensuring that AIoT deployments promote ethical aims and human well-being.

7.6.1 Human-Centric KPIs

Traditional KPIs focus on financial results, operational efficiency, and market share. However, by definition, AIoT systems have a direct influence on human experiences, whether in consumer encounters, staff processes, or community participation. Thus, human-centric KPIs aim to assess the qualitative components of AIoT adoption, such as customer happiness, trust, accessibility, and well-being [97]. For example, in client-facing AIoT applications such as smart retail or tailored healthcare, KPIs should include not only sales or operational efficiency but also customer happiness, user engagement, and emotional connection. These metrics are critical for assessing the human effect of AIoT solutions and ensuring that they provide a pleasant user experience that is consistent with the organization's overall values and objectives.

Human-centric KPIs in the workplace can focus on employee well-being and productivity while also considering how AIoT systems improve or disrupt workers' experiences. For example, AIoT in smart industries can improve employee safety by detecting hazards in real time, monitoring physical strain to prevent injury, and promoting ergonomic practices [98]. By focusing on worker health, safety, and happiness, organizations can guarantee that their AIoT projects encourage a more supportive, inclusive, and compassionate workplace.

Furthermore, accessibility becomes an important KPI when AIoT solutions are considered, especially for enterprises that service various clientele, including people with impairments. Ensuring that AIoT systems are inclusive, accessible, and simple to use for a diverse spectrum of individuals is critical for delivering fair customer experiences. For example, AIoT-powered smart home devices should be built to be easily accessible to elderly individuals or those with physical disabilities, thereby increasing their independence and quality of life [99].

7.6.2 Ethics-Driven ROI

While ROI has historically been solely a financial statistic, the integration of AIoT technologies necessitates a broader view of returns—one that takes into account ethical, social, and environmental factors. Ethics-driven ROI takes into account not only the financial benefits of AIoT investments but also their broader impact on ethical behaviors, social responsibility, and environmental sustainability [100]. Companies, for example, can calculate the ROI of AIoT activities by assessing sustainability benefits through resource optimization, such as energy savings from smart buildings or lower emissions from AI-enabled transportation systems [101].

Furthermore, AIoT ethics—particularly in terms of data protection, fairness, openness, and accountability—have become critical components of ROI. Ethical AI deployments prioritize data governance, ensuring that user data are gathered, kept, and processed with complete consent, transparency, and adherence to privacy standards such as the GDPR (General Data Protection Regulation) or CCPA (California Consumer Privacy Act). Measuring the ethical elements of AIoT ROI involves determining how effectively enterprises adhere to these principles, safeguarding user privacy, and preventing reinforcing biases in AI models, thereby guaranteeing that AIoT solutions do not harm people or communities.

In healthcare, for example, AIoT systems can enhance patient outcomes through real-time monitoring and predictive analytics. However, the ethical concerns of collecting and using patient data must be thoroughly explored. The ROI, in this situation, should assess not only gains in patient care but also how effectively the system complies with ethical norms, guarantees informed consent, and prevents prejudice. Ethics-driven ROI also includes promoting beneficial societal effects. Businesses should strive to create value not only for their shareholders but also for the communities they serve.

For example, in smart city efforts, AIoT solutions that optimize public transit systems, improve public health services, or increase safety and security contribute to community well-being. Improved public satisfaction, lower crime rates, and better access to key services may all be used to calculate the ROI of these programs [102]. Finally, human-centric KPIs and ethics-driven ROI represent a trend toward more holistic corporate measures that capture the broader effect of AIoT systems. These frameworks go beyond typical financial metrics to ensure that AIoT deployments are ethically sound, contribute to societal well-being, and promote human-centered outcomes.

As organizations progressively integrate AIoT technology into their operations, integrating these systems with human values and ethical standards will be crucial in developing sustainable, responsible, and successful digital transformations.

7.7 Strategic Sustainability for Long-Term Prosperity

As organizations increase their use of AIoT technologies, it is vital to assess how these systems contribute to long-term value generation and corporate sustainability. In the context of the AIoT, long-term value refers not only to financial returns but also to the long-term social, environmental, and economic impacts that the AIoT may have on a company and its stakeholders. Corporate sustainability entails creating company strategies that satisfy the requirement for balanced growth by emphasizing profit, environmental stewardship, and social responsibility. AIoT solutions, with their ability to optimize operations, improve decision-making, and stimulate innovation, play an important role in achieving these goals.

7.7.1 Long-Term Value Creation with AIoT

AIoT systems' long-term value is derived from their capacity to increase operational efficiency, develop business models, and improve consumer experiences. AIoT technology can improve process efficiency by automating repetitive operations, delivering real-time insights, and decreasing human error. In manufacturing, for example, AIoT-driven predictive maintenance may extend machinery life and minimize downtime, resulting in long-term cost savings and increased productivity. Over time, these efficiency gains enable organizations to remain competitive and resilient in a continually changing market.

Furthermore, AIoT solutions promote innovation by allowing organizations to build new goods and services that provide value to customers. In the healthcare industry, for example, AIoT-powered wearable devices provide real-time health monitoring, allowing for tailored treatment regimens and proactive health management. These creative solutions not only improve customer happiness and loyalty but also create new revenue sources, ensuring that organizations stay relevant and profitable in the long run. Furthermore, the data provided by AIoT systems provide important insights into customer behaviour, preferences, and industry trends. This plethora of information enables firms to make better educated, data-driven decisions that are consistent with long-term strategy objectives.

For example, AIoT analytics may assist firms in optimizing supply chain operations, properly forecasting demand, and identifying cost-cutting opportunities, resulting in long-term profitability. In this manner, the AIoT serves as a catalyst for organizational agility, allowing firms to respond swiftly to market changes and consumer demands.

7.7.2 Corporate Sustainability and the AIoT

AIoT technology also contributes to business sustainability by encouraging changes in environmental and social behaviors. Sustainable development is no longer a term; it is a strategic requirement for companies looking to prove their operations in the future. The AIoT may help organizations reduce their environmental impact by increasing energy efficiency, decreasing waste, and optimizing resources.

For example, AIoT solutions in smart buildings allow for automated control of lighting, heating, and cooling systems, decreasing energy consumption and carbon emissions. Similarly, in agriculture, AIoT-powered precision farming techniques improve water consumption, reduce pesticide application, and increase crop yields, all of which lead to more sustainable food production practices. Furthermore, the AIoT can improve social sustainability by increasing workplace safety, inclusiveness, and worker well-being. AIoT applications in various industries, including manufacturing and construction, employ sensors and real-time analytics to monitor worker health and safety and identify risks before accidents occur.

7.7 Strategic Sustainability for Long-Term Prosperity

Furthermore, AIoT technologies may promote inclusion by creating accessible solutions for individuals with impairments, hence increasing the social effect of company operations. Incorporating sustainability into company plans requires striking a balance between financial aims and larger societal objectives. When utilized properly, AIoT may assist organizations in striking this balance by integrating operational benefits with environmental and social objectives. The incorporation of sustainable AIoT activities into the business model guarantees that long-term value creation is focused not only on immediate profits but also on delivering beneficial societal and environmental consequences.

To summarize, long-term value and company sustainability are intrinsically intertwined in the context of AIoT implementation. Businesses that wisely use AIoT systems can provide long-term economic benefits while also addressing environmental and social concerns. The integration of the AIoT with business sustainability goals improves long-term profitability, boosts competitive advantage, and promotes good societal effects. To attain these goals, organizations must take a comprehensive strategy that includes ethical concerns, clear data governance, and an emphasis on innovation. As a result, the AIoT has become a powerful driver of long-term business practices that benefit both enterprises and society as a whole.

Chapter 8
Evolving Challenges, Trends and Future Directions

The artificial intelligence of things (AIoT) environment is rapidly evolving owing to technology breakthroughs and the integration of creative solutions from numerous sectors. This section explores the rising trends that shape AIoT adoption, providing an in-depth examination of each element.

Extension of Edge AI: The convergence of AI and edge computing is altering data processing paradigms by putting computations closer to the data source. Some applications require real-time data analysis and decision-making, which can be challenging because of the need for low-latency and high-speed data processing. The AIoT often relies on edge computing to process data locally on devices rather than in centralized data centers. Edge AI enables real-time analytics and decision-making while lowering latency and bandwidth use. Healthcare and manufacturing use edge AI to allow faster reactions and improve operational efficiency. For example, in healthcare, edge AI enables real-time patient monitoring and diagnosis, resulting in better patient outcomes. Managing AI models and updates at the edge introduces unique challenges in terms of device capabilities and maintenance. Balancing the energy efficiency of devices, especially at the edge, is critical for prolonging device lifespan and ensuring reliability, which is distinct from traditional AIoT concerns.

Further, managing hybrid AI models and optimizing their interactions adds complexity. Different applications may have varying tolerances for latency. Tailoring AI models and data processing to meet specific latency requirements is challenging. AIoT systems must adapt to and learn from evolving data patterns. The development of algorithms that can continually adapt to changing conditions and data inputs is a unique challenge. Many IoT devices have limited resources (e.g., memory and processing power), and AIoT solutions need to be tailored to operate within these constraints while delivering meaningful AI capabilities. Securing edge devices against physical and remote attacks presents is challenging because of the distributed nature of AIoT systems. It often involves decision-making distributed across multiple devices. Coordinating these decisions and ensuring that they align with broader objectives can be complex. IoT devices operate in dynamic and often unpredictable environments. Ensuring the robustness and reliability of systems under such conditions is a concern. Privacy concerns regarding data processed at the edge, where personal data may be more vulnerable, require unique privacy-preserving solutions. Developing industry standards for the AIoT, particularly with respect to AI models and processing at the edge, is an emerging challenge. Ensuring seamless and effective interaction between humans and AI at the edge is essential, given the distributed nature of the AIoT.

Adaptive Perception Technologies: Adaptive perception technologies are transforming AIoT systems by improving their capacity to comprehend and respond to a variety of external cues. AI-driven image signal processing (AI-ISP) is a remarkable achievement in this field since it greatly improves image quality under difficult settings. AI-ISP decreases noise and motion blur, allowing devices to shoot better photographs under low-light conditions. This innovation is especially useful for applications that need accurate visual data, such as surveillance, autonomous cars, and industrial automation.

Collaborative Ecosystems and Open Platforms: Due to the complexity of AIoT solutions, collaborative ecosystems and open platforms that foster interoperability and innovation are needed. Hikvision, for example, has developed frameworks such as HikFlow and HikStream to make it easier to integrate third-party algorithms into their systems. HikFlow helps adapt AI models to specific hardware, whereas HikStream optimizes the data flow, allowing developers to build AI-powered apps in a variety of industries, including retail, transportation, and security.

Emphasis on Cybersecurity: As the number of AIoT devices grows, it is critical to implement strong cybersecurity safeguards. The integration of AI and the IoT creates new risks, necessitating proactive threat detection and response tactics. Implementing sophisticated AI-driven cybersecurity solutions may help detect and mitigate attacks in real time, protecting critical data and ensuring system integrity.

Integration of 5G Networks: The deployment of 5G networks considerably improves AIoT capabilities by enabling quicker and more reliable data transfer. The enhanced bandwidth and lower latency of 5G technology enable complex applications such as autonomous driving, smart cities, and industrial automation, where massive amounts of data must be processed and transferred with precision and speed.

These developing trends highlight the revolutionary potential of the AIoT in a variety of domains. Staying on top of these changes is critical for enterprises looking to deploy AIoT technology successfully and sustainably.

The proposed future research directions are as follows:

- Augment the phased AIoT adoption strategy with real-world examples or case studies illustrating successful organizational implementations of each phase.
- The practical applicability of sociotechnical readiness guidelines should be enhanced by providing deeper insights into their implementation across diverse organizational contexts.

- Research robustness can be strengthened by integrating quantitative data, such as statistical analyses or survey results, to complement qualitative findings.
- Applicability can be increased by offering specific recommendations tailored to organizations at different stages of technological maturity, particularly those with limited resources.
- The significance of contextual factors can be recognized by providing more guidance on adapting sociotechnical readiness factors and guidelines to specific organizational contexts.
- The ethical dimensions of the AIoT can be delved deeper, to explore potential challenges and to propose practical strategies for their mitigation.

Chapter 9
Conclusions

The book covered a broad spectrum of the basics of the AIoT; benefits, frameworks, challenges and recommendations; seamless integration complexities; human-centric decision-making; and the need for privacy, security, and ethical adaptability in dynamic environments. The book first highlighted that successful AIoT adoption requires a strategic balance between technical proficiency and sociocultural considerations. The book then detailed the strategic AIoT adoption approaches and frameworks, which complement sociotechnical guidelines aligned with AIoT challenges. The guidelines emphasize the following:

- Clear objectives are crucial for successful integration and the alignment of strategies with organizational goals.
- Ethical considerations, change management, and regulatory compliance address sociocultural dimensions, emphasizing responsible implementation.
- Guidelines for iterative learning and feedback align with the evolving nature of AIoT systems, ensuring ongoing refinement.
- Risk assessment is embedded within the monitoring and maintenance phase, facilitating proactive identification and mitigation.
- Security and privacy form a fundamental layer, safeguarding data integrity and user privacy.

A sociotechnical approach based on AIoT implementation and management has various advantages that contribute to the overall success and sustainability of the AIoT. The benefits include:

- Increased user acceptance and satisfaction: Engaging stakeholders in the design and implementation of AIoT systems fosters a deeper understanding of user needs and preferences. This, in turn, ensures that AIoT systems are user friendly, effective, and aligned with user expectations.

- Improved collaboration and communication: Involving stakeholders from diverse departments and organizational levels breaks down silos and promotes collaboration. This collaborative approach ensures the seamless integration of AIoT systems into existing workflows, enhancing efficiency and productivity.
- Increased innovation and creativity: Tapping into the knowledge and expertise of employees, customers, and partners during the design and implementation phases stimulates innovation. This collaborative effort identifies new opportunities, fostering the development of innovative products, services, and business models.
- Increased sustainability and social responsibility: A sociotechnical approach ensures that environmental and social impacts are considered. Organizations can develop and implement AIoT systems responsibly and sustainably, contributing to long-term success and societal well-being.

By embracing a sociotechnical approach, organizations can not only optimize the technical aspects of AIoT adoption but also enhance user satisfaction, collaboration, and innovation and contribute to broader sustainability and social responsibility.

However, "communication and education" are vital recommendations for attaining sociotechnical readiness in AIoT adoption. Clear communication and educational initiatives are critical for informed decision-making. Effective communication is key to aligning all stakeholders involved in AIoT projects, from technical teams to business leaders and end-users. This ensures that everyone understands the goals, benefits, and implications of AIoT systems. Additionally, education plays a crucial role in empowering employees and stakeholders with the knowledge and skills needed to work with AIoT technologies effectively and ethically. This education should extend beyond the technical aspects and encompass the ethical considerations, data privacy concerns, and best practices associated with the AIoT. By fostering a culture of open communication and continuous learning, organizations can create a supportive environment that facilitates successful AIoT implementation, minimizes misunderstandings, and promotes responsible AIoT use, ultimately leading to business growth.

Appendix A
Glossary of Key Terms

Term	Definition
AIoT	The convergence of artificial intelligence (AI) and the internet of things (IoT), allowing devices to make intelligent decisions
Algorithmic bias	Systematic and unfair discrimination arises when AI models reflect historical inequalities or data imbalances. Managing bias is critical to ensure fair and inclusive AIoT outcomes
Cyber-physical systems	Systems that integrate computation with physical processes through embedded software and sensors
Digital twin	A virtual representation of a physical object or process used for real-time simulation and monitoring
Data sovereignty	The concept that data is subject to the laws and governance structures within the nation it is collected
Edge computing	A distributed computing paradigm where data is processed close to the source rather than relying on cloud infrastructure
Ethical AI framework	A set of principles and guidelines that govern responsible AI development, such as fairness, accountability, transparency, and nonmaleficence. Examples include the EU AI Act, IEEE ethically aligned design, and the AI4People framework
Explainable AI (XAI)	AI systems designed to provide human-understandable explanations for their outputs and decisions. It supports user trust, compliance, and accountability, especially in high-stakes domains like healthcare and finance
Human-centric AI	An approach to AI development and deployment that prioritizes human values, needs, agency, and well-being. It emphasizes transparency, fairness, explainability, and ethical alignment in algorithmic decision-making
Human-in-the-loop (HITL)	A system design approach where human operators are retained in decision-making cycles, either for supervision, validation, or intervention, ensuring that AI acts as an augmentative rather than autonomous agent

(continued)

(continued)

Term	Definition
Interoperability	The ability of systems and devices to work together using standardized protocols and formats
Sociotechnical systems	Systems that involve a complex interaction between humans, machines, and organizational environments. The term acknowledges that successful technology implementation must address both social (cultural, psychological, ethical) and technical dimensions

Appendix B
AIoT Readiness Assessment Checklist

A practical checklist for organizations evaluating their readiness to adopt AIoT solutions.

Area	Assessment questions	Status
Strategic alignment	Does AIoT align with organizational goals and digital strategy?	☐ Yes ☐ No
Infrastructure	Do we have the necessary connectivity, hardware, and computing capabilities?	☐ Yes ☐ No
Data management	Are data governance, storage, and processing systems in place?	☐ Yes ☐ No
Talent and skills	Do we have access to AI, IoT, and data analytics expertise?	☐ Yes ☐ No
Cross-functional collaboration	Are departments collaborating on digital initiatives?	☐ Yes ☐ No
Risk management and compliance	Are security, privacy, and regulatory considerations embedded into the process?	☐ Yes ☐ No
Ethical and social considerations	Have we accounted for ethical AI use, potential biases, and job implications?	☐ Yes ☐ No

Appendix C
Examples of Human-Centric KPIs for AIoT Systems

This appendix provides sample KPIs to help organizations move beyond traditional metrics and evaluate the human impact of AIoT systems. KPIs should be collected both quantitatively (surveys, behavioral analytics) and qualitatively (interviews, ethnographic methods) and then integrated into regular reporting dashboards.

Domain	Traditional KPI	Human-centric KPI
Smart retail	Footfall, conversion rates	Customer delight index (based on feedback/sentiment)
Healthcare IoT	Treatment efficiency	Patient experience scores, inclusivity index
Smart manufacturing	Uptime, output per hour	Worker satisfaction, ergonomic risk scores
Smart cities	Traffic flow rate	Pedestrian safety and accessibility compliance
Remote monitoring	Sensor uptime	End-user trust in automated alerts

Appendix D
Ethical AIoT Implementation Checklist

This checklist is intended for practitioners to evaluate whether AIoT systems meet ethical design and deployment standards. Organizations can use this checklist during project planning, piloting, and audits to ensure compliance with both internal values and external regulations (e.g., GDPR, ISO/IEC 42001).

Category	Checklist Item	✓/✗
Fairness	Have bias audits been conducted on datasets?	☐
	Are outputs tested across demographics for equity?	☐
Transparency	Are AI decisions explainable to end users?	☐
	Is there a communication plan for data usage policies?	☐
Accountability	Are there clear lines of responsibility for AI outputs?	☐
Privacy	Is consent-based data collection implemented?	☐
	Is sensitive data encrypted and protected at all levels?	☐
User autonomy	Are users able to override or contest AI decisions?	☐
Environmental impact	Is energy consumption monitored and optimized?	☐

Appendix E
Regulatory Landscape

Region	Key AIoT-related regulations
European Union	GDPR, AI Act (proposed), ePrivacy Regulation
United States	CCPA, NIST AI Risk Management Framework, FTC IoT Guidelines
China	Cybersecurity Law, Personal Information Protection Law (PIPL), AI Standards Roadmap
India	Digital Personal Data Protection Act 2023, Draft National Strategy for AI and IoT
Global bodies	IEEE Standards Association, ISO/IEC JTC 1/SC 42 AI and IoT standards

Appendix F
Tools and Platforms for AIoT Development

Tool/platform	Function	Description
AWS IoT Core	IoT management platform	Connects devices and routes data to cloud applications securely
Microsoft Azure AI and IoT Hub	Integrated AIoT platform	Provides prebuilt services for edge intelligence, device management, and ML
TensorFlow Lite	AI model deployment on edge devices	Optimized AI inference engine for mobile and embedded IoT devices
OpenHAB	Open-source smart automation	Platform for integrating diverse IoT systems using a common interface
ThingSpeak	IoT analytics and visualization	Allows real-time data visualization and MATLAB analytics for IoT devices

References

1. T.W. Sung, P.W. Tsai, T. Gaber, and C.Y. Lee, "Artificial Intelligence of Things (AIoT) technologies and applications", Wireless Communications and Mobile Computing, vol. 2021, Aug. 2021, Art. no. 9781271. https://doi.org/10.1155/2021/9781271.
2. Forecast Analysis: Artificial Intelligence Software, 2023–2027, Worldwide. https://www.gartner.com/en/documents/4916331, 2023 (accessed 21 Jan 2025).
3. 54% of the companies have implemented AI for business: PwC India survey, https://www.pwc.in/press-releases/2023/54-of-the-companies-have-implemented-ai-for-business-pwc-india-survey.html, 2023 (accessed 27 Jan 2025).
4. State of IoT – Spring 2023. https://iot-analytics.com/product/state-of-iot-spring-2023/, 2023 (accessed 31 March 2024).
5. T. Shenkoya, "Social change: A comparative analysis of the impact of the IoT in Japan, Germany and Australia", Internet of Things, vol. 11, Art. no. 100250, Sep. 2020, https://doi.org/10.1016/j.iot.2020.100250.
6. Chung KC, Tan PJ. Artificial intelligence and internet of things to improve smart hospitality services. Internet of Things. Vol. 31, Article. No. 101544, Feb 2025. https://doi.org/10.1016/j.iot.2025.101544
7. K.M. Hou, X. Diao, H. Shi, H. Ding, H. Zhou, and C. de Vaulx, "Trends and Challenges in AIoT/IIoT/IoT Implementation", Sensors, vol. 23, no. 11, p. 5074, May 2023, https://doi.org/10.3390/s23115074.
8. M. Ge, H. Bangui, and B. Buhnova, "Big data for internet of things: A survey", Future Generation Computer Systems, vol. 87, pp. 601–614, Oct 2018, https://doi.org/10.1016/j.future.2018.04.053.
9. Z. Lv, L. Qiao, and S. Verma, "AI-enabled IoT-edge data analytics for connected living", ACM Transactions on Internet Technology, vol. 21, no. 4, 104, pp. 1–20, July 2021, https://doi.org/10.1145/3421510.
10. Z. Chang, S. Liu, X. Xiong, Z. Cai, and G. Tu, "A survey of recent advances in edge-computing-powered artificial intelligence of things", IEEE Internet of Things Journal, vol. 8, no. 18, pp. 13849–13875, Sept. 2021, https://doi.org/10.1109/JIOT.2021.3088875.
11. Siam, S. I., Ahn, H., Liu, L., Alam, S., Shen, H., Cao, Z., ... & Zhang, M. "Artificial intelligence of things: A survey", *ACM Transactions on Sensor Networks*, vol. *21*, No. 1, pp. 1–75., Jan 2025. https://doi.org/10.1145/3690639
12. C.C. Byers and P. Wetterwald, "Fog computing distributing data and intelligence for resiliency and scale necessary for IoT, The internet of things (ubiquity symposium)", Ubiquity, vol. 2015, no. 4, pp. 1–12, Nov 2015, https://doi.org/10.1145/2822875.

13. D. Wang, D. Chen, B. Song, N. Guizani, X. Yu, and X. Du, "From IoT to 5G I-IoT: The next generation IoT-based intelligent algorithms and 5G technologies", IEEE Communications Magazine, vol. 56, no. 10, pp. 114–120, Oct. 2018, https://doi.org/10.1109/MCOM.2018.1701310.
14. A.M. Zarca, J.B. Bernabe, A. Skarmeta, and J.M.A.Calero, "Virtual IoT HoneyNets to mitigate cyberattacks in SDN/NFV-enabled IoT networks", IEEE Journal on Selected Areas in Communications, vol. 38, no. 6, pp. 1262–1277, June 2020, https://doi.org/10.1109/JSAC.2020.2986621.
15. A. Siddiqi, H. Yu, and J. Joung, "5G ultra-reliable low-latency communication implementation challenges and operational issues with IoT devices", Electronics, vol. 8, no. 9, 981, Sept. 2019, https://doi.org/10.3390/electronics8090981.
16. C. Li, Y. Peng, G. Liu, Y Li, X. Yang, Z. Luochuan, and C. Chen, "Efficient vision transformer for human-centric AIoT applications through token tracking assignment", IEEE Transactions on Consumer Electronics, Early Access, Oct 2023, https://doi.org/10.1109/TCE.2023.3323373.
17. S. Islam, A.K. Budati, M.K. Hasan, S.B. Goyal, and A. Khanna, "Performance analysis of video data transmission for telemedicine applications with 5G enabled Internet of Things", Computers and Electrical Engineering, vol. 108, Art. no. 108712, May 2023, https://doi.org/10.1016/j.compeleceng.2023.108712
18. C. Wang, C. W. Liao, K.P.Lin, C.H.Wang, and C.L.Tsai, "Evaluate the consumer acceptance of AIoT-based unmanned convenience stores based on perceived risks and technological acceptance models", Mathematical Problems in Engineering, Art. no. 4416270, pp. 1–12, July 2021, https://doi.org/10.1155/2021/4416270.
19. Rosca CM, Rădulescu G, Stancu A. "Artificial Intelligence of Things Infrastructure for Quality Control in Cast Manufacturing Environments Shedding Light on Industry Changes" Applied Sciences. Vol. 15, No. 4, Article. 2068, Jan 2025. https://doi.org/10.3390/app15042068
20. A. Matin, M.R. Islam, X. Wang, H. Huo, and G. Xu, "AIoT for sustainable manufacturing: Overview, challenges, and opportunities", Internet of Things, vol. 24, Art. no. 100901, Dec 2023, https://doi.org/10.1016/j.iot.2023.100901
21. Shell to use new AI technology in deep sea oil exploration. https://energy.economictimes.indiatimes.com/news/oil-and-gas/shell-to-use-new-ai-technology-in-deep-sea-oil-exploration/100294138, 2023 (accessed 1 October 2024).
22. H.T. Wu, "The internet-of-vehicle traffic condition system developed by artificial intelligence of things", The Journal of Supercomputing, vol. 78, no. 2, pp. 2665–2680, Feb. 2022, https://doi.org/10.1007/s11227-021-03969-0.
23. M.K. Gowri, "Impact of the Internet of Things (IoT) on Logistics", Journal of Image Processing and Intelligent Remote Sensing, vol. 3, no. 1, pp. 1–10, Jan 2023, https://doi.org/10.55529/jipirs.31.1.10.
24. S.D. Mooney, "Technology platforms and approaches for building and evaluating machine learning methods in Healthcare", The Journal of Applied Laboratory Medicine, vol. 8, no. 1, pp. 194–202, Jan 2023, https://doi.org/10.1093/jalm/jfac113.
25. Transforming Airport Operations: Leveraging AI for Facilities Management. https://www.aviationpros.com/airports/article/55056209/transforming-airport-operations-leveraging-ai-for-facilities-management, 2024 (accessed 1 Feb 2025).
26. A.K Nair, C. John, and J. Sahoo, "Implementation of intelligent IoT", in AI and IoT for Sustainable Development in Emerging Countries: Challenges and Opportunities, Cham: Springer International Publishing, Jan 2022, vol. 104, pp. 27–50, https://doi.org/10.1007/978-3-030-90618-4_2
27. W.T. Sung, S.J. Hsiao, and C.Y. Hsiao, "Constructing a deep image analysis system based on self-driving and AIoT", Intelligent Automation & Soft Computing, vol. 31, no. 2, Feb 2022, pp. 1223–1240, https://doi.org/10.32604/iasc.2022.020746.
28. V. Bhardwaj, R. Joshi, and A.M. Gaur, "IoT-based smart health monitoring system for COVID-19", SN Computer Science, vol. 3, Art. no. 137, pp. 1–11, Jan 2022, https://doi.org/10.1007/s42979-022-01015-1.

References

29. A.J. Perez, F. Siddiqui, S. Zeadally, and D. Lane, "A review of IoT systems to enable independence for the elderly and disabled individuals", Internet of Things, vol. 21, Art. no. 100653, pp. 1–23, April 2023, https://doi.org/10.1016/j.iot.2022.100653.
30. B. Muangmeesri and K. Wisaeng, "IoT-based discomfort monitoring and a precise point positioning technique system for smart wheelchairs", Applied System Innovation, vol. 5, no. 5, Art. no. 103, pp. 1–15, Oct. 2022, https://doi.org/10.3390/asi5050103.
31. M. Gupta, R. K. Jha and S. Jain, "Tactile based intelligence touch technology in IoT configured WCN in B5G/6G-A survey", IEEE Access, vol. 11, pp. 30639–30689, Feb. 2023, https://doi.org/10.1109/ACCESS.2022.3148473.
32. N.K. Rout, S. Das, S. Saxena, and P. Ghosh, "IoT-Based Smart Farming Using AI", AI to Improve e-Governance and Eminence of Life: Kalyanathon 2020, Springer Nature Singapore, Sep 2023, vol. 130, pp. 59–88, https://doi.org/10.1007/978-981-99-4677-8_4.
33. C.J. Chen, Y.Y. Huang, Y.S. Li, C.Y. Chang, and Y.M. Huang, "An AIoT based smart agricultural system for pests detection", IEEE Access, vol. 8, pp. 180750–180761, Sep 2020, https://doi.org/10.1109/ACCESS.2020.3024891.
34. B.L.R. Stojkoska and K.V. Trivodaliev, "A review of Internet of Things for smart home: Challenges and solutions", Journal of Cleaner Production, vol. 140, pp. 1454–1464, Jan 2017, https://doi.org/10.1016/j.jclepro.2016.10.006.
35. Y.H. Kuo and E.H.K. Wu, "Advanced, innovative AIoT and edge computing for unmanned vehicle systems in factories", Electronics, vol. 12, no. 8, pp. 1843, April 2023, https://doi.org/10.3390/electronics12081843.
36. A. Alzuhair, and A. Alghaihab, "The design and optimization of an acoustic and ambient sensing AIoT platform for agricultural applications", Sensors, vol. 23, no. 14, Art. no. 6262, pp. 1–11, July 2023, https://doi.org/10.3390/s23146262
37. H.K. Adli et al., "Recent advancements and challenges of AIoT application in smart agriculture: A review", Sensors, vol. 23, no. 7, Art. no. 3752, April 2023, https://doi.org/10.3390/s23073752
38. E.S. Bibri, J. Krogstie, A. Kaboli, and A. Alahi, "Smarter eco-cities and their leading-edge artificial intelligence of things solutions for environmental sustainability: A comprehensive systematic review", Environmental Science and Ecotechnology, vol. 19, Art. No. 100330, May 2024, https://doi.org/10.1016/j.ese.2023.100330
39. A. Pise, B. Yoon, and S.Singh, "Enabling Ambient Intelligence of Things (AIoT) healthcare system architectures," Computer Communications, vol. 198, pp. 186–194, Jan 2023, https://doi.org/10.1016/j.comcom.2022.10.029.
40. F. Zhang, Z. Pan, and Y. Lu, "AIoT-Enabled smart surveillance for personal data digitalization: Contextual personalization-privacy paradox in smart home", Information & Management, vol. 60, no. 2, Art. no. 103736, Mar. 2023, https://doi.org/10.1016/j.im.2022.103736
41. A. Sleem, and I. Elhenawy, "Survey of Artificial Intelligence of Things for Smart Buildings: A closer outlook", Journal of Intelligent Systems & Internet of Things, vol. 8, no. 2, pp. 63–71, 2023, https://doi.org/10.54216/jisiot.080206.
42. K. Brecker, S. Lins, and A. Sunyaev, "Why it remains challenging to assess artificial intelligence," in proceedings of the 56th Hawaii Conference on System Sciences (HICSS), Maui, Hawaii, Jan. 2023, pp. 5242–5251, https://doi.org/10.5445/IR/1000154715.
43. E.B. Kang, "Ground truth tracings (GTT): On the epistemic limits of machine learning", Big Data & Society, vol. 10, no. 1, pp. 1–12, Jan. 2023, https://doi.org/10.1177/20539517221146122.
44. What is the main source of unresolved machine learning ethical concerns. https://cs.unu.edu/news/news/ml-ethical-concerns.html, 2023 (accessed 4 Feb 2025).
45. A. Rawal, J. McCoy, D. B. Rawat, B. Sadler, and R.S. Amant, "Recent advances in trustworthy explainable artificial intelligence", IEEE Transactions on Artificial Intelligence, vol. 3, no. 6, Dec 2021, https://doi.org/10.1109/TAI.2021.3133846.
46. H. Vella, "Smart abuse: who controls the controls?", Engineering & Technology, vol. 13, no. 6, pp. 44–47, July 2018, https://doi.org/10.1049/et.2018.0603.

47. How can digital rights defenders respond to the rising use of government hacking as the Internet of Things grows? https://digitalfreedomfund.org, 2023 (accessed 1 Feb 2025).
48. S.C. Kong, W.M.Y. Cheung, and G. Zhang, "Evaluating artificial intelligence literacy courses for fostering conceptual learning, literacy and empowerment in university students: Refocusing to conceptual building", Computers in Human Behavior Reports, vol. 7, Art. no. 100223, Aug 2022, https://doi.org/10.1016/j.chbr.2022.100223.
49. When algorithms decide and regulating those decisions. https://www.orfonline.org/expert-speak/when-algorithms-decide-and-regulating-those-decisions, 2023 (accessed 24 May 2024).
50. N. Shadbolt, K. O'Hara, T. Berners-Lee, N. Gibbins, H. Glaser, W. Hall, and M.C. Schraefel, "Linked open government data: Lessons from Data.gov.uk", IEEE Intelligent Systems, vol. 27, no. 3, pp. 16–24, May–June 2012, https://doi.org/10.1109/MIS.2012.23.
51. M. S. Kamal, N. Dey, L. Chowdhury, S. I. Hasan, K. Santosh, "Explainable AI for Glaucoma prediction analysis to understand risk factors in treatment planning", IEEE Transactions on Instrumentation and Measurement, vol. 71, no. 2509209, pp. 1–9, 2022, https://doi.org/10.1109/TIM.2022.3171613.
52. S. Fong, N. Dey and A. Joshi, "ICT Analysis and Applications", Lecture Notes in Networks and Systems, vol. 154, pp. 715–730, Springer Nature Singapore, 2020, https://doi.org/10.1007/978-981-15-8354-4.
53. P. Brous and M. Janssen, "A systematic review of impediments blocking internet of things adoption by governments", Open and Big Data Management and Innovation, I3E 2015, Lecture Notes in Computer Science, vol. 9373, Springer, pp. 81–94, Nov. 2015, https://doi.org/10.1007/978-3-319-25013-7_7.
54. N. Guhr, O. Werth, P.P.H. Blacha, and M.H. Breitner, "Privacy concerns in the smart home context", SN Applied Sciences, vol. 2, pp. 1–12, Jan 2020, https://doi.org/10.1007/s42452-020-2025-8.
55. N. Dey, A. S. Ashour, and C. Bhatt, "Internet of things driven connected healthcare", Internet of Things and Big Data Technologies for Next Generation Healthcare, Springer: Cham, Switzerland, pp. 3–12, Jan 2017, https://doi.org/10.1007/978-3-319-49736-5_1
56. T. Dhar, N. Dey, S. Borra, and R.S. Sherratt, "Challenges of deep learning in medical image analysis-improving explainability and trust", IEEE Transactions on Technology and Society, vol. 4, no. 1, pp. 68–75, Mar. 2023, https://doi.org/10.1109/TTS.2023.3234203.
57. H. de Bruijn, M. Warnier, and M. Janssen, "The perils and pitfalls of explainable AI," Government Information Quarterly, vol. 39, no. 2, 101666, April 2022, https://doi.org/10.1016/j.giq.2021.101666.
58. R. Yu and G. Alì, "What's inside the black box?", AI Challenges for Lawyers and Researchers, Legal Information Management, vol. 19, no. 1, pp. 2–13. April 2019, https://doi.org/10.1017/S1472669619000021.
59. Creating an inclusive digital future - urgent action needed. https://digitalfreedomfund.org/creating-an-inclusive-digital-future-urgent-action-needed (accessed 2 October 2024).
60. P. Brous, M. Janssen and P. Herder, "The dual effects of the Internet of Things (IoT): A systematic review of the benefits and risks of IoT adoption by organizations", International Journal of Information Management, vol. 51, Art. no. 101952, April 2020, https://doi.org/10.1016/j.ijinfomgt.2019.05.008.
61. J. Contreras-Castillo, S. Zeadally, and J. A. Guerrero-Ibañez, "Internet of vehicles: Architecture, protocols, and security", IEEE Internet of Things Journal, vol. 5, no. 5, pp. 3701–3709, Oct 2018, https://doi.org/10.1109/JIOT.2017.2690902.
62. L. Nicholls, Y. Strengers, and J. Sadowski, "Social impacts and control in the smart home", Nature Energy, vol. 5, no. 3, pp. 180–182, March 2020, https://doi.org/10.1038/s41560-020-0574-0.
63. I. Tuomi, "A framework for socio-developmental ethics in educational AI", in Proceedings of the 56th Hawaii International Conference on System Science, Maui, Hawaii, 2023, vol. 6, pp. 6208–6217, https://hdl.handle.net/10125/103386.

64. J. Mökander and L. Floridi, "Ethics-based auditing to develop trustworthy AI", Minds & Machines, vol. 31, no. 2, pp. 323–327, June 2021, https://doi.org/10.1007/s11023-021-09557-8.
65. M. O'Neill, "The Internet of Things: do more devices mean more risks?", Computer Fraud & Security, vol. 2014, no. 1, pp. 16–17, Jan 2014, https://doi.org/10.1016/S1361-3723(14)70008-9.
66. F. Zampati, "Ethical and Legal Considerations in Smart Farming: A Farmer's Perspective", Towards Responsible Plant Data Linkage: Data Challenges for Agricultural Research and Development, Springer, Cham, 2023, pp. 257–272, https://doi.org/10.1007/978-3-031-13276-6_13.
67. E.E. Makarius, D. Mukherjee, J.D. Fox, A.K. Fox, "Rising with the machines: A sociotechnical framework for bringing artificial intelligence into the organization," Journal of Business Research, Elsevier, vol. 120(C), pp. 262–273, Aug 2020, https://doi.org/10.1016/j.jbusres.2020.07.045
68. B. Shneiderman, "Human-centered artificial intelligence: Reliable, safe & trustworthy", International Journal of Human–Computer Interaction, vol. 36, No. 6, pp. 495–504, 2020.
69. F. Morandín-Ahuerma, "Recommendation of the OECD council on artificial intelligence: inequality and inclusion", 1. CC BY-NC-SA, pp. 95–102, 2023
70. M. Cannarsa, "Ethics guidelines for trustworthy AI", The Cambridge handbook of lawyering in the digital age", pp. 283–297, 2021.
71. A.Rai, "Explainable AI: From black box to glass box", Journal of the academy of marketing science, 48, 1, pp. 137–141, 2020.
72. S. Costanza-Chock, "Design justice: Community-led practices to build the worlds we need". The MIT Press, 2020
73. S Zuboff, S., 2019. The age of surveillance capitalism. PublicAffairs. *New York*.
74. A. Cavoukian, "Privacy by design: The 7 foundational principles". *Information and privacy commissioner of Ontario, Canada, 5*(2009), p. 12.
75. Friedman, B. and Hendry, D.G., 2019. *Value sensitive design: Shaping technology with moral imagination*. MIT Press.
76. Ozay, Dervis, Mohammad Jahanbakht, Atefeh Shoomal, and Shouyi Wang. "Artificial Intelligence (AI)-based Customer Relationship Management (CRM): a comprehensive bibliometric and systematic literature review with outlook on future research." *Enterprise Information Systems* 18, no. 7 (2024): 2351869.
77. Kamboj, S. and Rana, S., 2023. Big data-driven supply chain and performance: a resource-based view. *The TQM Journal, 35*(1), pp. 5–23.
78. Akter, S., Bandara, R., Hani, U., Wamba, S.F., Foropon, C. and Papadopoulos, T., 2019. Analytics-based decision-making for service systems: A qualitative study and agenda for future research. *International Journal of Information Management, 48*, pp. 85–95.
79. Lee, I. and Lee, K., 2015. The Internet of Things (IoT): Applications, investments, and challenges for enterprises. *Business horizons, 58*(4), pp. 431–440.
80. Porter, M.E. and Heppelmann, J.E., 2015. How smart, connected products are transforming companies. *Harvard business review, 93*(10), pp. 96–114.
81. Shin, D., 2021. The effects of explainability and causability on perception, trust, and acceptance: Implications for explainable AI. *International journal of human-computer studies, 146*, p. 102551.
82. Vashishth, T.K., Sharma, V., Sharma, K.K., Sharma, R. and Sharma, M.K., 2025. Affective Computing in Social Robotics. In *Humanizing Technology With Emotional Intelligence* (pp. 361–384). IGI Global Scientific Publishing.
83. Darabkh, K.A. and Al-Akhras, M., 2025. Evolutionary Cost Analysis and Computational Intelligence for Energy Efficiency in Internet of Things-Enabled Smart Cities: Multi-Sensor Data Fusion and Resilience to Link and Device Failures. *Smart Cities, 8*(2), p. 64.
84. Lee, J., & Riek, L. D. (2018). Reframing assistive robots to promote successful aging. *ACM Transactions on Human-Robot Interaction (THRI), 7*(1), 1–23.

85. Yin, X., Lam, H. K., & Zhang, Y. (2021). Emotion-aware AI systems for customer service: A systematic review. *Computers in Human Behavior Reports*, 3, 100070.
86. Tocchetti, A., Corti, L., Balayn, A., Yurrita, M., Lippmann, P., Brambilla, M. and Yang, J., 2025. Ai robustness: a human-centered perspective on technological challenges and opportunities. *ACM Computing Surveys*, 57(6), pp. 1–38.
87. Amershi, S., Cakmak, M., Knox, W. B., & Kulesza, T. (2014). Power to the people: The role of humans in interactive machine learning. *AI Magazine*, 35(4), 105–120.
88. Xu, X., Lu, Y., Vogel-Heuser, B. and Wang, L., 2021. Industry 4.0 and Industry 5.0—Inception, conception and perception. *Journal of manufacturing systems*, 61, pp. 530–535.
89. Ng, I.C. and Wakenshaw, S.Y., 2017. The Internet-of-Things: Review and research directions. *International Journal of Research in Marketing*, 34(1), pp. 3–21.
90. Tao, F., Qi, Q., Liu, A. and Kusiak, A., 2018. Data-driven smart manufacturing. *Journal of manufacturing systems*, 48, pp. 157–169.
91. Verhoef, P.C., Kannan, P.K. and Inman, J.J., 2015. From multi-channel retailing to omnichannel retailing: introduction to the special issue on multi-channel retailing. *Journal of retailing*, 91(2), pp. 174–181.
92. Atzori, L., Iera, A. and Morabito, G., 2010. The internet of things: A survey. *Computer networks*, 54(15), pp. 2787–2805.
93. Sutskever, I., Vinyals, O., & Le, Q. V. (2014). Sequence to sequence learning with neural networks. *Advances in Neural Information Processing Systems*, 27, 3104–3112.
94. Lipton, Z.C., 2018. The mythos of model interpretability: In machine learning, the concept of interpretability is both important and slippery. *Queue*, 16(3), pp. 31–57.
95. Venkatraman, N. (2019). The digital transformation of business models in the industrial sector. *MIS Quarterly Executive*, 18(3), 149–168.
96. Hess, T., Matt, C., Benlian, A., & Wiesböck, F. (2016). Options for formulating a digital transformation strategy. *MIS Quarterly Executive*, 15(2), 123–139.
97. Shneiderman, B., 2020. Human-centered artificial intelligence: Three fresh ideas. *AIS Transactions on Human-Computer Interaction*, 12(3), pp. 109–124.
98. Rathod, S.B., Mahajan, R.A., Khadkikar, P.A., Vyawahare, H.R. and Patil, P.R., 2024. Improving workplace safety with AI-powered predictive analytics: enhancing workplace security. In *AI Tools and Applications for Women's Safety* (pp. 232–249). IGI Global Scientific Publishing.
99. Fakhimi, M.M., Hughes, A. and Gustavson, A.M., 2025. Evaluating Smart Home Usability and Accessibility in Early Detection and Intervention of Mental Health Challenges Among Older Adults: A Narrative Review and Framework. *Journal of Ageing and Longevity*, 5(1), p. 3.
100. Jorzik, P., Klein, S.P., Kanbach, D.K. and Kraus, S., 2024. AI-driven business model innovation: A systematic review and research agenda. *Journal of business research*, 182, p. 114764.
101. Zainol, Z., Brotosaputro, G., Chen, S.C. and Natasya, E.A., 2025. Designing Ethical AI Systems for Sustainable Technology Development. *ADI Journal on Recent Innovation*, 6(2), pp. 201–211.
102. Batty, M., Axhausen, K.W., Giannotti, F., Pozdnoukhov, A., Bazzani, A., Wachowicz, M., Ouzounis, G. and Portugali, Y., 2012. Smart cities of the future. *The European Physical Journal Special Topics*, 214, pp. 481–518.

If you have any concerns about our products,
you can contact us on
ProductSafety@springernature.com

In case Publisher is established outside the EU,
the EU authorized representative is:
**Springer Nature Customer Service Center GmbH
Europaplatz 3, 69115 Heidelberg, Germany**

Printed by Libri Plureos GmbH
in Hamburg, Germany